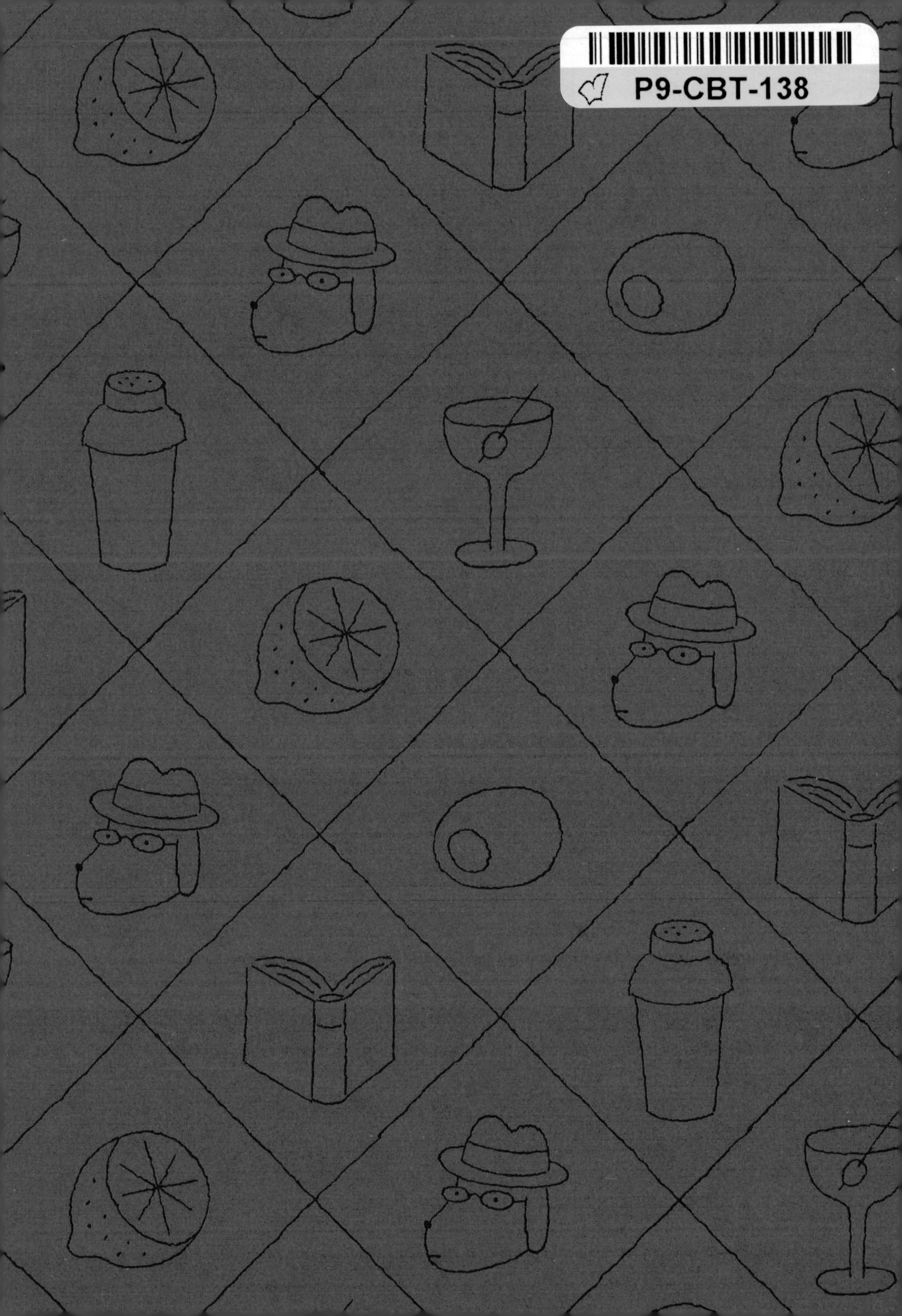

A SIDECAR
NAMED DESIRE

A SIDECAR NAMED DESIRE

Great Writers and the Booze That Stirred Them

Greg Clarke and Monte Beauchamp

DEY ST.
An Imprint of WILLIAM MORROW

DEY ST.

A SIDECAR NAMED DESIRE. Copyright © 2018 by Greg Clarke and Monte Beauchamp. All rights reserved. Printed in the United States of America. No part of this book may be used or reproduced in any manner whatsoever without written permission except in the case of brief quotations embodied in critical articles and reviews. For information, address HarperCollins Publishers, 195 Broadway, New York, NY 10007.

HarperCollins books may be purchased for educational, business, or sales promotional use. For information, please email the Special Markets Department at SPsales@harpercollins.com.

FIRST EDITION

Designed by Janet Evans-Scanlon

Library of Congress Cataloging-in-Publication Data has been applied for.

ISBN 978-0-06-269638-0

18 19 20 21 22 LSC 10 9 8 7 6 5 4 3 2 1

To Jenifer, Greta, and Julian.
　　—Greg Clarke

For Rebecca Ann, who keeps me
believing in impossible things.
　　—Monte Beauchamp

CONTENTS

Prologue

WHEN THE SPIRITS MOVE YOU

As I say, I was lighted up. In my brain every thought was at home. Every thought, in its little cell, crouched ready-dressed at the door, like prisoners at midnight, waiting a jail-break. And every thought was a vision, bright-imaged, sharp-cut, unmistakable. My brain was illuminated by the clear, white light of alcohol. John Barleycorn was on a truth-telling rampage. . . . And I was his spokesman.

—Jack London, *John Barleycorn* (1913)

Humankind has been turning to booze to help summon up creative inspiration since before the days of Bacchus. The history of alcohol, and its use by writers, artists, and musicians to stimulate the imagination and elicit the elusive muse, is well documented. Temperance zealots over the years may have decried the evils of drink, but there are considerable examples in the canon of literature to suggest, at the very least, a connection between alcohol and great writing.

In the case of some writers, the eventual toll booze exacted on mind and body was significant, and access to the muse short-lived. Jack London, Malcolm Lowry, Ernest Hemingway, F. Scott Fitzgerald, Edna St. Vincent Millay, and Jack Kerouac all soared to great heights under the influence, only to crash and burn. Other writers—James Joyce, Herman Melville, Maya Angelou—managed to reap the creative benefits of alcohol's mind-loosening properties without succumbing to its ravages.

A 2012 study reported in the journal *Consciousness and Cognition* (conducted by Andrew F. Jarosz, Gregory J. H. Colflesh, and Jennifer Wiley, at the University of Illinois at Chicago) supports the notion that thinking "outside the box"—a necessary precondition for creativity—can be aided by a few drinks. In "Uncorking the Muse: Alcohol Intoxication Facilitates Creative Problem Solving," the authors share their finding that sober subjects took longer to solve creative word problems than their tipsy counterparts.

In addition to alcohol's creative benefits, we would argue that there is no greater pleasure than a good book, paired with a good drink! Certain writers, and certain bottles of alcohol, now fetch eye-popping sums on the auction block. Recently, ten bottles of 1945 Château Mouton Rothschild Bordeaux sold for $343,000, while an inscribed 1925 first edition of Fitzgerald's *The Great Gatsby* sold for $162,500. Proof positive that we like our booze, and we like our authors who like their booze.

Perhaps unsurprisingly, the idea for this book, a history of spirits and great literature accompanied by copious visual tomfoolery, was conceived in a dimly lit bar following a tough week at the studio—and the consumption of several rejuvenating sidecars. Two years and many cocktails later, the Muse of Booze has blessed us with this book. Cheers!

—*Monte Beauchamp* and *Greg Clarke*, October 2018

WINE

Chapter 1

Wine is bottled poetry.

—Robert Louis Stevenson, *The Silverado Squatters* (1884)

Booze-ologists may quibble over which spirit is older, beer or wine, but there's no question that wine has inspired more rapturous poetry and prose. Great literature aside, wine has inspired a cottage industry of scribes who make their living writing exclusively about the beverage. Picture the oft-derided wine critic with the golden palate, capable of detecting hints of pencil lead, saddle leather, road tar, cigar box, cat piss, and wet dog in his glass.

Regardless of which came first, it was undoubtedly a happy accident when Stone Age hominids discovered the intoxicating properties of spoiled, or naturally fermented, fruit juice. They couldn't possibly know that what they were drinking would ultimately stir the human imagination, grease the wheels of civilization, and become the most widely written about liquid refreshment in human history.

ANCIENT GEORGIA ON MY MIND

Many historians consider ancient Georgia to be the birthplace of wine. Inhabitants of the fertile valleys of the South Caucasus have been making wine for eight thousand years using an age-old method that requires no wooden barrels, vats, or monitoring systems. Instead, they used (and still use today) giant terra-cotta *qvevri* vessels made from Georgian clay and lined with beeswax.

The pots were buried underground and filled with grapes, which were then fermented with natural yeast for two weeks and sealed for six to twelve months of aging.

The Georgian national poet, Shota Rustaveli, was among the earliest native sons to sing the praises of the region's wines. His twelfth-century epic poem, *The Knight in the Panther's Skin* (written some two hundred years before Thomas Malory's *Le Morte d'Arthur*), is a story of knights, friendship, chivalry, and courtly love, filled with references to the local wine culture.

Shota Rustaveli.

WILD GRAPES IN CHINESE ANTIQUITY

In ancient China, a fermented beverage using indigenous Chinese grapes appeared in the prehistoric Neolithic era, around 7000 BC, but larger-scale production of grape wine didn't happen until the Tang dynasty (AD 618–907).

Tang dynasty silver cup.

In his poem "Xiuxi Yin," Eastern Han dynasty poet Ruan Ji (210–263) wrote, in a testament to wine as a creative stimulant, "Once drunk, a cup of wine can bring 100 stanzas of poetry."

Ruan Ji.

Li Bai (701–762), considered one of China's greatest poets, wrote rapturously of wine— one of his most famous poems is entitled "Waking from Drunkenness on a Spring Day." He would later die drunk, drowning facedown in a river while attempting to embrace the moon's reflection.

5

PERSIAN WINE OF YORE

Recent excavations in Iran (ancient Persia) have uncovered pottery vessels containing tartaric acid, an indicator of the presence of wine, dating from 3100–2900 BC.

Ancient Persian drinking vessel.

According to Persian folklore, wine was discovered when a girl, despondent after being rejected by her king, attempted suicide by poisoning herself with the residue of rotted grapes. Her spirits were miraculously lifted, and the next day she reported her intoxicating discovery to the king, who duly rewarded her.

Twelfth-century Persian poet and philosopher Omar Khayyám's verse is soaked in references to wine and the joy it brings to our fleeting existence on earth. In *The Rubáiyát*, the title given to a selection of his poems translated by poet Edward FitzGerald and published in 1859, Khayyam writes:

Omar Khayyám.

> Drink wine. This is life eternal.
> This is all that youth will give you.
> It is the season for wine,
> roses and drunken friends.
> Be happy for this moment.
> This moment is your life.

Later, in the fourteenth century, Persian Sufi poet Hafiz wrote of wine as a symbol of love and the divine. Here are several stanzas from his collection *Drunk on the Wine of the Beloved: 100 Poems of Hafiz*, translated by Thomas Rain Crowe:

> *From the large jug, drink the wine of Unity,*
> *So that from your heart you can wash away*
> *the futility of life's grief.*

Hafiz.

But like this large jug, still keep the heart expansive.
Why would you want to keep the heart captive,
like an unopened bottle of wine?

With your mouth full of wine, you are selfless
And will never boast of your own abilities again.

Even though, to the pious, drinking wine is a sin,
Don't judge me; I use it as a bleach to wash the color
of hypocrisy away.

DRINKING WITH THE PHARAOHS

Viniculture dates back to 3100 BC in the Nile Delta, where wine was mostly consumed at the court of the pharaohs and by the upper classes. Members of the Egyptian ruling class were often entombed with a large stash of wine to ease the journey to the afterlife.

Chemical analysis of the residue left in a jar recovered from King Tut's tomb indicates that he had a preference for red wine. His many wine jars were labeled with the vineyard source, the name of the chief vintner, and the year the wine was made.

The Egyptians shared their knowledge of wine with the Phoenicians, who would then spread it around the world.

ODE TO A GRECIAN FLAGON OF WINE

Wine arrived in Greece via Phoenician sailors crossing the Mediterranean around 1200 BC. It played an important role in ancient Greek culture, and its glories were extolled in verse and song. Dionysus (aka Bacchus to the Romans) was their god of the vine.

For the Greek philosophers, wine and philosophy were inseparable—the symposia were more like wine parties where philosophical discussion took place. As Plato once said, "No thing more excellent nor more valuable than wine was ever granted mankind by God."

Wine is frequently mentioned in the work of Greek playwright Aristophanes, who considered it a boon to creativity. In his play *The Knights* (424 BC), the character Demosthenes requests "a flagon of wine, that I may soak my brain and say something clever."

On the civilizing influence of wine, Thucydides, the Greek historian, observed, "The peoples of the Mediterranean began to emerge from barbarism when they learnt to cultivate the olive and the vine."

Thucydides.

IN VINO VERITAS

The Roman Empire picked up where the Greeks left off, perfecting the winemaking process and establishing virtually all the major wine-producing regions that exist in western Europe today. They were the first to use barrels (borrowed from the Gauls) and glass bottles (borrowed from the Syrians), rather than earthenware vessels, for storage and shipping.

Ancient Roman wine jug.

The Roman poet Virgil, writing down instructions to wine growers, dispensed a key bit of advice that still holds today: "Vines love an open hill."

Pliny the Elder with Roman drinking horn.

Pliny the Elder, the first-century naturalist and author of the thirty-seven-volume encyclopedia *Naturalis historia*, wrote extensively on viticulture, including a ranking of the "first growths" of Rome, and introducing the concept of terroir (that a particular region's climate, soil, and terrain imparts unique characteristics to the taste of a wine). Pliny is also the source of the most famous Latin proverb on wine: "In vino veritas" (In wine there is truth).

Horace, the Roman poet, was devoted to wine. When contemplating his death, he expressed more heartache over departing from his wine cellar than from his wife. Regarding poetic inspiration, he wrote, "Poems written by water drinkers will never enjoy long life or acclaim."

THE MERRY BARD OF AVON

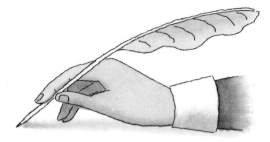

Good company, good wine, good welcome can make good people. . . .
—Henry VIII, act 1, scene 4

In William Shakespeare's England (1564–1616), wine was very expensive—about twelve times more costly than ale, the drink of the masses—and typically enjoyed only by the upper classes. England's climate was not suitable for growing grapes, so most of its wine was imported from France, Spain, and Greece. Sack, a sweet wine fortified with brandy (akin to modern-day sherry) was also very popular during the Elizabethan era.

. . . man cannot make him laugh—but that's no marvel; he drinks no wine.
—Henry IV, part 2, act 2, scene 4

The wine of life is drawn, and the mere lees Is left this vault to brag of.
—Macbeth, act 2, scene 3

Little is known of Shakespeare's personal drinking habits, but as a man of means, he could undoubtedly afford to drink something other than ale. By all accounts, he was not the sodden party animal of his contemporary Christopher Marlowe, but the frequent wine cameos in his work suggest he probably enjoyed it. His characters cite many more wine varieties—muscatel, Rhine, Bordeaux, canary, and malmsey—than they do ale or beer.

Give me a bowl of wine. In this I bury all unkindness . . .
—Julius Caesar, act 4, scene 3

Have we no wine here?
—Coriolanus, act 1, scene 9

I am falser than vows made in wine.
—*As You Like It*, act 3, scene 5

Good wine is a good familiar
creature, if it be well used . . .
—*Othello*, act 2, scene 3

O thou invisible spirit of wine,
if thou hast no name to be
known by, let us call thee devil!
—*Othello*, act 2, scene 3

ALL THE WORLD'S A STAGE FOR WINE

And let my liver rather heat with wine,
Than my heart cool with mortifying groans.
—*The Merchant of Venice*, act 1, scene 1

VIVE LE VIN FRANÇAISE!

France, blessed with soil and climate conditions ideally suited for viticulture, has long reigned as the world's greatest purveyor of fine wine (only to be challenged in the latter half of the twentieth century by California). Its two predominant wine regions, Bordeaux and Burgundy, produce some of the most famous and expensive wines that we consume today.

During a visit to Bordeaux in 1787, Thomas Jefferson—America's first wine connoisseur—placed orders for 24 cases of Château Haut-Brion, 250 bottles of Château Lafite, and an unspecified amount of Château d'Yquem.

Thomas Jefferson.

In 1855, Emperor Napoleon III suggested a classification system in Bordeaux to identify the region's best wines. Known as the Bordeaux Wine Official Classification of 1855, the rankings established so-called first through fifth growths and remain largely unchanged to this day.

Emperor Napoleon III.

Roald Dahl.

Modern Bordeaux and Burgundy lovers can be counted among the literary elite . . .

British author Roald Dahl, of *Charlie and the Chocolate Factory* (1964) fame, made wine the subject of a short story that appeared in *The New Yorker* in 1951. "Taste" is the tale of a bet on wine vintages at a London dinner party. Dahl was an avid wine collector with a keen interest in Bordeaux and Burgundy, and a particular obsession with Bordeaux from 1982 (regarded by many as the greatest vintage of modern times).

Peter De Vries.

Comic novelist and *New Yorker* contributor Peter De Vries called himself a "winebibber" and was especially enamored of the wines of Burgundy: "The masculine *Montrachet* and the feminine *Musigny* offer the most exquisite communion with earth, air and sky open to man." The witticism "Write drunk, edit sober," which seems to have gone viral, is often attributed to Ernest Hemingway. But in fact it can be traced to De Vries. A character in his novel *Reuben, Reuben* (1964) says,

"Sometimes I write drunk and revise sober, and sometimes I write sober and revise drunk. But you have to have both elements in creation."

THE MACABRE OENOPHILE

The nineteenth-century poet Lord Byron, author of the satiric poem *Don Juan* (1819), is known for having fashioned a drinking vessel out of a

human skull that his gardener uncovered at his ancestral home, Newstead Abbey, in Nottinghamshire, England. He was borrowing a tradition dating back to Gaulish chieftains using Roman skulls as drinking goblets. Byron sent the well-preserved skull to town and reported that "it returned with a very high polish, and of a mottled colour like tortoiseshell."

Lord Byron.

Byron had a poem inscribed on the side of the skull, prosaically titled "Lines Inscribed Upon a Cup Formed from a Skull." In it, he meditates on the mind's nobler purpose in death—as a bony receptacle from which the living can enjoy the splendors of claret (the British term for red wine from Bordeaux): "And when, alas! our brains are gone, What nobler substitute than wine?"

Charles Baudelaire.

THE ADDLED OENOPHILE

When not exploring altered states of consciousness in opium dens or hashish clubs, Charles Baudelaire, the French poet, essayist, and art critic, always defaulted to wine as his intoxicant of choice.

In his 1851 essay "Du vin et du haschish" ("On Wine and Hashish"), he asks, "Who has not known the profound joys of wine? Everyone who has ever had remorse to appease, a memory to evoke, a grief to drown, a castle in Spain to build—in short, *everyone*—has invoked the mysterious god hidden in the fibres of the vine."

NASCENT NAPA VALLEY

In 1880 the soon-to-be famous Scottish author of *Treasure Island* (1883), Robert Louis Stevenson, honeymooned in Napa Valley. In *The Silverado Squatters* (1884), an account of his time there at the dawn of California's wine industry, he describes the trial-and-error process of planting grapes: "Wine in California is still in the experimental stage. . . . One corner of land after another is tried with one kind of grape after another. This is failure; that is better; a third best. So, bit by bit, they grope about for their Clos Vougeot and Lafite."

Robert Louis Stevenson.

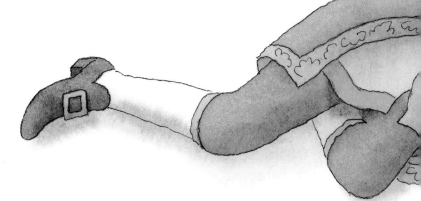

DAVID VERSUS GOLIATH:
The Judgment of Paris

Father Junípero Serra.

A Franciscan missionary, Father Junípero Serra, planted California's first sustained vineyard at Mission San Diego de Alcalá in 1779. Following the publication of *The Silverado Squatters*, the state's wine industry had been on a long, slow climb toward respectability, with sporadic triumphs along the way.

But the pivotal turning point in the history of California wine would occur on May 24, 1976. In the so-called Judgment of Paris, a wine competition organized by a British wine merchant, a cluster of California upstart wines dethroned their renowned Bordeaux and Burgundy counterparts in a blind tasting. In a blow to French wine supremacy, Napa Valley had arrived as one of the world's great wine regions.

PAPA AND THE GRAPE

Ernest Hemingway is arguably the most iconic literary figure in booze lore. Hemingway was—to use a term that H. L. Mencken originally coined for himself—"ombibulous." He drank everything and enjoyed it all.

Following the horrors of World War I, many disillusioned American writers, feeling that the arts had become increasingly underappreciated at home, emigrated to Europe as part of the "Lost Generation." Hemingway was among them, arriving in Paris in 1921 to work as a foreign correspondent for the *Toronto Star*. It was here, in close proximity to Bordeaux and Burgundy, that his introduction to fine wine likely occurred.

In *A Moveable Feast* (1964), his memoir of life in Paris, he recounts a meal at home with his then wife, Hadley, in which, too poor to eat out, they drink "Beaune from the co-operative." Beaune is the capital city of Burgundy, France's great wine region. And it's likely that even Beaune from a Parisian co-op was not half-bad.

16

The prodigious drinking that occurs in his 1926 novel *The Sun Also Rises* can be viewed as Hemingway's repudiation of Prohibition in the United States. The story's narrator, American expatriate Jake Barnes, and his circle of friends travel from Paris, France, to Pamplona, Spain, to watch the running of the bulls and the bullfights. In chapter 15 alone, seven liters of wine are shared between three people.

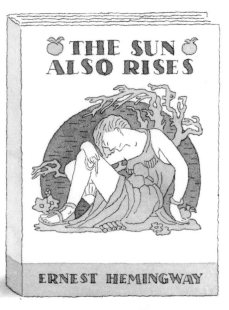

THE SUN ALSO RISES

ERNEST HEMINGWAY

The classic French laguiole pocketknife with a corkscrew has been in use since 1880.

Hemingway and his characters didn't mind the slower pace and fewer complications of drinking alone, either. At one point Jake says, "I drank a bottle of wine for company. It was a Château Margaux. It was pleasant to be drinking slowly and to be tasting the wine and to be drinking alone. A bottle of wine was good company."

In his paean to Spanish bullfighting, *Death in the Afternoon* (1932), Hemingway writes: "Wine is one of the most civilized things in the world and one of the most natural things of the world that has been brought to the greatest perfection, and it offers a greater range for enjoyment and appreciation than, possibly, any other purely sensory thing."

HAVE WINE, WILL TRAVEL

Many writers with a taste for adventure have fallen prey to wine's allure. British author D. H. Lawrence traveled extensively throughout Italy, France, Mexico, the United States, and Australia, sampling wines along the way. But the author of *Lady Chatterley's Lover* (1928) did not love all that he tasted, and he could be an unforgiving critic. He once described a Spanish wine as "the sulphurous urination of some aged horse."

James Joyce's favorite wine was Fendant de Sion, a fruity Swiss white made from the Chasselas grape. He must have discovered the varietal while living off and on in Zurich, Switzerland, where he wrote much of *Ulysses* (1922) and would later finish writing *Finnegans Wake* (1939).

D. H. Lawrence.

James Joyce.

In *Finnegans Wake*, he likens the wine to the urine of an archduchess (apparently high praise!), referring to it in Joycean code as "Fanny Urinia."

18

M. F. K. Fisher, the doyen of American food writing and author of *How to Cook a Wolf* (1942), spent four years as a young woman living in Dijon, France, the culinary capital of Burgundy. There she was inculcated with the glories of French food and wine.

Fisher could be effusive on the subject of wine. In the preface to *The University of California/Sotheby Book of California Wine* (1984) she writes: "I can no more think of my own life without thinking of wine and wines and where they grew for me and why I drank them when I did and why I picked the grapes and where I opened the oldest procurable bottles, and all that, than I can remember living before I breathed."

M. F. K. Fisher.

The French novelist Marguerite Duras was born abroad. The daughter of two teachers, she spent her childhood in French Indochina (now Vietnam) before returning to her parents' native country at age seventeen. Duras has said that she wrote her popular novel *The Lover* (1984) when she was drunk. Speaking to the *New York Times* in 1991, she commented on alcohol's role in her daily routine, "I drank red wine to fall asleep. . . . Every hour a glass of wine and in the morning Cognac after coffee, and afterwards I wrote. What is astonishing when I look back is how I managed to write."

BUKOWSKI'S BROMANCE

Charles Bukowski.

In a 1994 interview with *Transit* magazine, Charles Bukowski declared, "As a young man, I hung around the libraries during the day and the bars at night." When asked to describe his ideal conditions for writing, he responded, "Between 10 p.m. and 2 a.m. Bottle of wine, smokes, radio on to classical music. I write 2 or 3 nights a week."

In *Ham on Rye* (1982), his alter ego, Henry Chinaski, extolls the virtues of intoxication: "Getting drunk was good. I decided that I would always like getting drunk. It took away the obvious and maybe if you could get away from the obvious often enough, you wouldn't become obvious yourself."

When times were lean, Bukowski drank cheap beer, whiskey, or vodka. But when flush with royalty checks, he switched to fine red wine. Good wine was, according to Bukowski, "blood of the gods . . . the best for creation. You can write three or four hours."

Bukowski had long maintained a writing crush on John Fante, an obscure writer who had garnered critical acclaim with his early novels set in Los Angeles. But Fante's work, first published in the 1930s, never found an audience, and the author spent much of his life working in Hollywood as a screenwriter. As a young man, Bukowski had discovered Fante's books in the Los Angeles Public Library, and they were revelatory. "Fante was my god," he said.

Bukowski's last "typer," an IBM Selectric.

Fante's reputation enjoyed a renaissance after Bukowski sent a copy of *Ask the Dust* (1939) to his editor, John Martin, at Black Sparrow Press. Martin was so impressed that he set out to republish all of Fante's works, starting with *Ask the Dust* in 1980.

Wine, an integral part of Fante's Italian American upbringing, figured heavily in his work. He described his novel *The Brotherhood of the Grape* (1977) as "the story of four Italian wine drunks from Roseville, a tale revolving around my father and his friends."

The downtown LA dive bar frequented by both Bukowski and John Fante.

21

THERE'S SOMETHING ABOUT SHERRY

Sherry has a small, but fervent, following among certain writers . . .

The fortified white wine from Andalusia, Spain, plays a titular role in Edgar Allan Poe's short story "The Cask of Amontillado" (1846). The unhinged narrator lures an unwitting victim into his home for a sip of the wine, intent on killing him over a perceived slight that happened fifty years before. Amontillado is a darker sherry variety hailing from the Montilla region of Spain.

Sherry, mixed with hot tea, was Carson McCullers's drink of choice. The author of *The Heart Is a Lonely Hunter* (1940) dubbed the concoction a "Sonnie Boy." So as not to be conspicuous, she drank it from a thermos throughout the day while working at her typewriter. Her thermos was a constant companion during her most productive years.

Carson McCullers.

American poet and memoirist Maya Angelou, acclaimed for her 1969 autobiography *I Know Why the Caged Bird Sings*, was also a fan. In a 1983 interview she enumerated her essential items for a successful writing session: "I keep a dictionary, a Bible, a deck of cards and a bottle of sherry in the room."

Maya Angelou.

THE NOVELIST AS WINE WRITER

Jay McInerney, best known for *Bright Lights, Big City* (1984), has parlayed his passion for the grape into a sideline as a respected, if unorthodox, wine writer. Injecting new life into an increasingly stilted body of wine criticism, he has written monthly wine columns for *House & Garden* and *Town & Country* magazines. In his collection of essays, *A Hedonist in the Cellar: Adventures in Wine* (2006), he writes that "fermented grape juice is a far more potent catalyst for contemplation and meditation than a highball. . . . It is a sacramental beverage, a sacred and symbolic liquid."

He often eschews the usual floral descriptors in favor of cultural references. He's more apt to equate wine with authors and thespians than with sandalwood and pencil lead: "Bordeaux was my first love. . . . But increasingly I'm drawn to its rival Burgundy, the Turgenev to Bordeaux's Tolstoy, and when I'm looking for sheer power and exuberance and less finesse, to the Dostoyevskian southern Rhône."

McInerney on California Syrah: "Syrah . . . keeps threatening to become a California star, but so far its career has been a little like that of the actor Orlando Bloom, more promising than happening."

McInerney's beloved Château Haut-Brion: "the first growth of poets and lovers."

THE GLORIES OF BACCHUS

What is it about wine, relative to other spirits, that has inspired such a disproportionate amount of hand-scrawled veneration? Part of its allure, aside from taste bud friendliness (it's certainly easier to like than stronger, throat-scorching distillates), may be its inscrutability. Wine mutates in the bottle. Every wine is a moving target. The same sublime Châteauneuf-du-Pape you drank seven years ago might be plonk today. And as widely consumed as it is, no alcoholic beverage intimidates like wine—the sheer number of grape varietals, styles, and wine regions is bewildering. Thankfully, an ancillary industry of "experts" is out there to help, from wine critics who advise on the best bottles to buy to restaurant sommeliers whose highly trained noses will help you sniff out what to drink with your dinner.

Perhaps McInerney encapsulates the mystique of the beverage best when he writes that wine "can provide intellectual as well as sensual pleasure; it's an inexhaustible subject, a nexus of sub-jects, which leads us, if we choose to follow, into the realms of geology, botany, meteorology, history, aesthetics, and literature."

BEER

Chapter 2

I leant against the bar, between an alderman and a solicitor, drinking bitter.
. . . I liked the taste of beer, its live, white lather, its brass-bright depths, the sudden world through the wet brown walls of the glass, the tilted rush to the lips and the slow swallowing down to the lapping belly, the salt on the tongue, the foam at the corners.

—Dylan Thomas, "Old Garbo," *Portrait of the Artist as a Young Dog* (1940)

Unlike other spirits that have been up and down the socioeconomic ladder over the centuries, buffeted by history and changing tastes, beer has largely remained true to its working-class roots. Beer is most commonly made from malted barley, which is heartier and less susceptible to the whims of nature—bad weather and pest infestations—than the grapevine, making it easier, and cheaper, to produce.

Vintage brass bottle opener circa 1930s.

1940s cone-top beer can.

As such, beer has never enjoyed the exalted reputation of wine, and there hasn't been the ink devoted to it that there has been to its vinous cousin. But its origins reach back just as far, and it is the most widely consumed beverage in the world after water and tea. Some would even argue that the complexity and sophistication of a modern microbrew can rival that of a fine wine.

26

EARLY BEER: AMBER WAVES OF SPOILED GRAIN

Beer's beginnings likely coincided with the early transition of nomadic tribes to grain-based agrarian societies, likely going as far back as 10,000 BC. Some scholars have even suggested it was the advent of beer that turned early humans from foragers to farmers. The discovery of natural fermentation, which led to beer being brewed from cereal grains like barley, as well as wheat, corn, and rice, was undoubtedly accidental—the consequence of moist baked bread starting to spoil. In its earliest form, it was made with water and malted grain that was slowly fermented, or brewed. Hops would be introduced centuries later as a preserving agent and flavor enhancer.

Barley.

From antiquity to the late nineteenth century, beer was often a safer alternative to the unsanitary water from rivers and streams, and consequently consumed by men, women, and children alike.

Ancient Mesopotamian gold beer cup with drinking spout.

SUMERIAN SUDS

Archeological evidence of barley beer production dates back to the Sumerians of ancient Mesopotamia (modern-day Iran), between 3500 and 3100 BC. Cuneiform texts found at the Godin Tepe settlement, along the ancient Silk Road trading route, feature numerous pictographs of beer.

To filter out barley hulls and other debris, ancient Sumerians drank beer through straws made from gold or reeds.

The Epic of Gilgamesh (2700 BC), a Sumerian poem that is often considered the earliest surviving work of great literature, provides the first written account of beer as a source of merriment. In the poem a wild man named Enkidu is educated in the ways of men by Shamhat, a prostitute:

> "Eat the food, Enkidu, it is the way one lives.
> Drink the beer, as is the custom of the land."
> Enkidu ate the food until he was sated,
> He drank the beer—seven jugs!—and became
> expansive and sang with joy!

The *Hymn to Ninkasi* (circa 1800 BC) is an ode to the Sumerian goddess of beer, and includes a description of the brewing process. Literacy was uncommon at the time, and thus singing the hymn was a way to memorize and disseminate the recipe. The priestesses of Ninkasi are generally regarded as history's first brewers. Women were typically responsible for brewing in the home and often worked as tavern keepers as well. All levels of society consumed the beverage.

In the Old Testament's book of Genesis, Noah took measures to ease the boredom of forty days and forty nights of rain. His provisions list for the ark included barrels of Sumerian beer.

Ninkasi.

THE BEER-AMIDS

In ancient Egypt, beer similarly soaked through the fabric of daily life. Laborers received beer rations three times a day and were often compensated with beer for their work. And as in Mesopotamia, brewing was largely the provenance of women.

Like the Sumerians, the Egyptians regarded beer as a gift from the gods and believed that human beings had been taught to brew by the god Osiris. An inscription in the Dendera Temple complex from 2200 BC reads, "The mouth of a perfectly contented man is filled with beer."

HISTORY'S FIRST INSUFFERABLE WINE SNOBS

Both the ancient Greeks and Romans liked to deride beer as inferior to its beloved grape-based counterpart. Writing about the German predilection for beer, the Roman historian Tacitus could barely contain his contempt, "To drink, the Teutons have a horrible brew fermented from barley or wheat, a brew which has only a very far removed similarity to wine."

Sophocles.

Despite this snobbery, beer was still widely consumed in ancient Greece and Rome. The Greek playwright Sophocles advocated a daily diet of bread, meat, green vegetables, and beer. Excavations of an AD 179 Roman military encampment built by Marcus Aurelius on the Danube have uncovered evidence of large-scale beer brewing.

ZICKE, ZACKE, ZICKE, ZACKE, HOI, HOI, HOI

The Germans began brewing beer as early as 800 BC, but it wasn't until the Christian era that the beverage truly flourished. In the early Middle Ages, beer production in Europe became centralized in monasteries and convents. This provided not only hospitality for traveling pilgrims but also sustenance for monks during fasting.

Around AD 1150, German monks introduced hops to the brewing process, thus creating the revolutionary precursor to modern beer. Hops (the flowers of the hop plant), added a spiky, citric bitterness to counter the sweetness of the malt.

The German beer stein, with its hinged lid, originated in the fourteenth century following the bubonic plague and a series of insect invasions. By the early 1500s, German law required beverage containers to be covered as a sanitary measure.

JOHN BARLEYCORN

"John Barleycorn" is an English folk song of unknown origins that dates back to the sixteenth century. The titular character is a metaphor for barley. The song details Barleycorn's suffering and death at the hands of the farmer and the miller, corresponding to the different stages of barley cultivation (sowing, reaping, and malting). In death, this sacrificial figure is resurrected and his body, or blood, consumed in the form of beer and whiskey. Some scholars suggest that "John Barleycorn" was a pagan analog of Christian transubstantiation.

Many versions of "John Barleycorn" exist, but the most famous may be the ballad by Scottish poet Robert Burns, penned in 1782. In the final stanzas of the poem, he seems to be referring to beer, whiskey, or both:

> *John Barleycorn was a hero bold,*
> *Of noble enterprise;*
> *For if you do but taste his blood,*
> *'Twill make your courage rise.*

English ceramic "John Barleycorn" jug, circa 1934.

'Twill make a man forget his woe;
'Twill heighten all his joy;
'Twill make the widow's heart to sing,
Tho' the tear were in her eye.

Then let us toast John Barleycorn,
Each man a glass in hand;
And may his great posterity
Ne'er fail in old Scotland!

In 1913, Jack London would borrow "John Barleycorn" as the title for what he dubbed his "alcoholic memoirs," which chronicle both his love of drinking and his struggles with it: "He is the august companion with whom one walks with the gods. He is also in league with the Noseless One [death]."

London writes of getting drunk for the first time at the age of five, drinking beer from a bucket he was carrying to his stepfather at work in the fields. By the time he was in his teens, he could drink most men under the table. Early in his career as a writer, he refused to drink until he had written his thousand words a day. But that resolve slowly deteriorated, along with his health, over time. Later he had trouble writing without a drink, or as he called it, being "pleasantly jingled."

Jack London: portrait of the artist as a young beer drinker.

The first edition in its original dustwrapper.

London floridly describes his inebriated state: "As I say, I was lighted up. In my brain every thought was at home. Every thought, in its little cell, crouched ready-dressed at the door, like prisoners at midnight waiting a jail-break. And every thought was a vision, bright-imaged, sharp-cut, unmistakable. My brain was illuminated by the clear, white light of alcohol. John Barleycorn was on a truth-telling rampage, giving away the choicest secrets on himself. And I was his spokesman."

THE BREWMASTER OF HAMPSHIRE COUNTY

Jane Austen was not only a beer drinker but a brewer as well. Brewing was deemed a household duty for women in eighteenth-century England, and Austen likely learned the process as a teenager from her mother while growing up in the Hampshire village of Steventon. In a letter to her sister, Cassandra, in 1808, Austen writes: "It is you, however, in this instance, that have little children, and I that have the great cask, for we are brewing spruce beer again." Translation: You bring the kids, I've got the refreshments.

Spruce beer was akin to root beer (traditionally made from the roots and bark of the sassafras tree) but flavored instead with the buds, needles, and roots of the spruce tree, and containing hops and molasses. The Austen family clearly enjoyed their alcoholic beverages—they also brewed mead, a beer variation made by fermenting honey with water, and made wine.

Austen's brew makes an appearance in her novel *Emma* (1815): "He wanted to make a memorandum in his pocket-book; it was about spruce-beer. Mr. Knightley had been telling him something about brewing spruce-beer."

Austen's exact recipe has unfortunately been lost to history, but the Jane Austen Centre in Bath, England, offers an approximation:

Jane Austen's Spruce Beer

5 gallons water
⅛ pound hops
½ cup dried, bruised gingerroot
1 pound outer twigs of spruce fir
3 quarts molasses
½ yeast cake dissolved in ½ cup warm water

In a large kettle, combine the water, hops, gingerroot, and spruce fir twigs. Boil together until all the hops sink to the bottom of the kettle. Strain into a large crock and stir in the molasses. After this has cooled, add the yeast. Cover and leave to set for 48 hours. Then bottle, cap, and leave in a warm place (70–75°F) for five days, after which it will be ready to drink. Store upright in a cool place.

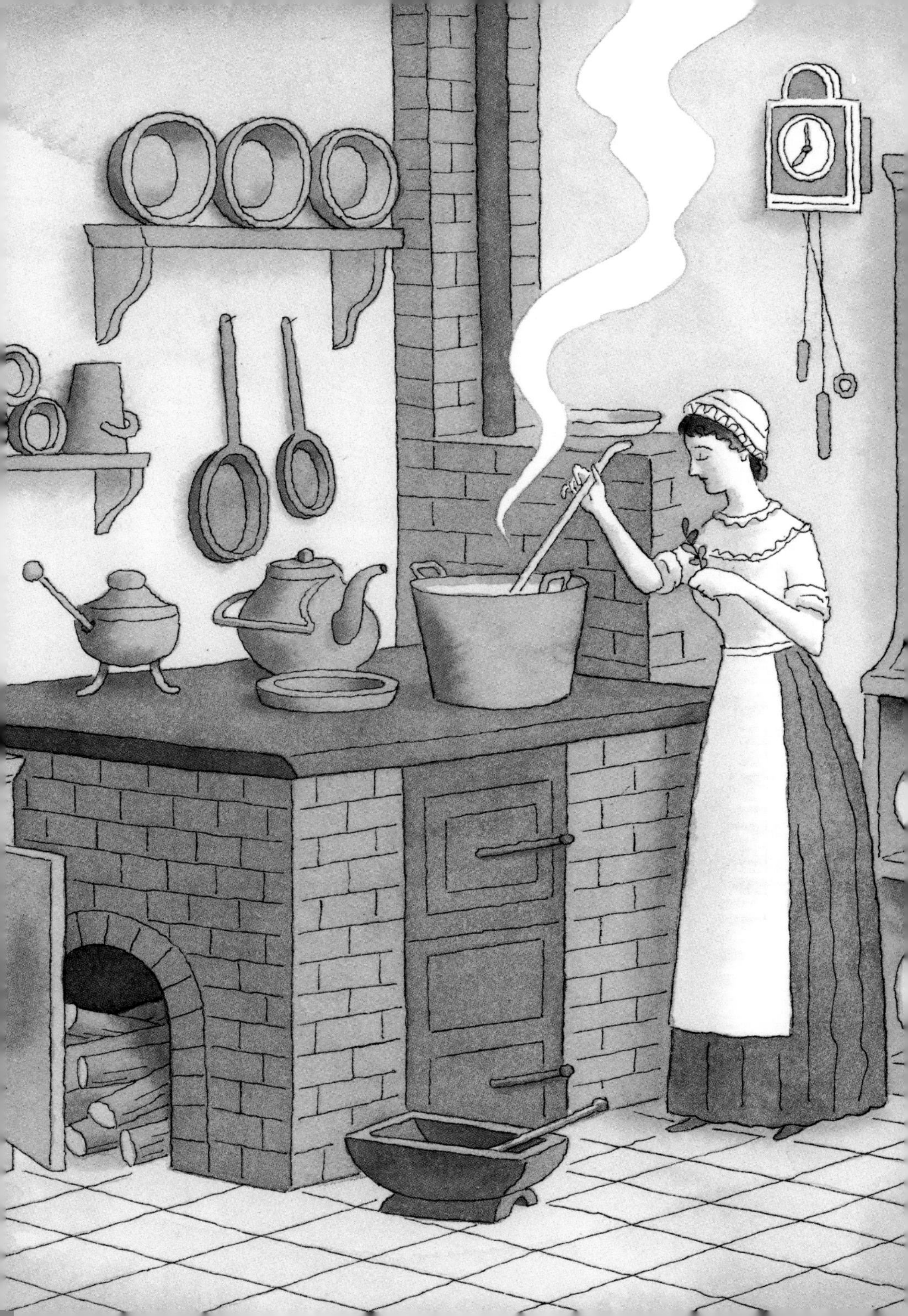

CRAFT BREWS: HOPPY DAYS ARE HERE AGAIN

George Hodgson.

The catalyst for the American craft-brewing revolution of the latter quarter of the twentieth century, a movement that would fundamentally alter the course of the beer industry, was the resurrection of an all-but-forgotten beer style— India pale ale, better known as IPA. Today's hop freaks owe an enormous debt of gratitude to Englishman George Hodgson, the eighteenth-century brewer widely credited for its creation.

The London brewery Hodgson's of Bow was founded in 1752 and situated on the river Lea, a convenient location for supplying beer to the East India Company's fleet at Blackwall on the river Thames. The East India Company was an English trading concern and chief provider of beer, and other goods, for the British Empire in the East. In the 1780s, Hodgson's revelation was to add dry hops as a preserving agent to the finished beer barrels, which helped prevent spoilage during the six-month sea voyages to the colonies in India. The sturdy new brew was dubbed India pale ale.

British author William Makepeace Thackeray came by his fondness for IPA naturally—he was born in India, where his father happened to work for the East India Company. He name-checks Hodgson's of Bow in his satirical novel set in colonial India, *The Tremendous Adventures of Major Gahagan* (first serialized in 1838): "It amused him, he said, to see me drink Hodgson's pale ale (I drank two hundred and thirty-four dozen the first year I was in Bengal)."

In the 1820s, Samuel Allsopp created his own version of Hodgson's "India ale."

Thackeray also alludes to Hodgson's in his most famous novel, *Vanity Fair* (1848), when an East India Company employee, Jos Sedley, imbibes "some of the ale for which the place is famous." And in his *Notes on a Journey from Cornhill to Cairo* (1846), Thackeray was ecstatic to discover "a camel-load of Hodson's [*sic*] pale ale from Beyroot [*sic*]."

William Makepeace Thackeray.

By the late nineteenth century, the advent of industrial refrigeration killed much of the IPA's raison d'être. Hops were no longer necessary for increased shelf life, giving way to the light lager styles that would gain favor and predominate for the next hundred years. However, hops would later return with a vengeance, in the form of America's craft brewing boom. West Coast breweries vying to out-hop one another would result in double and triple IPAs.

Hop flower.

VICTORIAN ERA "BOTTLED WATER"

The novels of Charles Dickens, the great social chronicler of his age, are suffused with beer, pub, and brewery references. Children in the nineteenth century, as reflected in Dickens's novels, drank "small beer" or "table beer," as a less toxic alternative to the unsanitary water of the Thames. The butler in *Dombey and Son* (1848), when serving sickly Paul Dombey junior "sometimes mingled porter with his table beer to make him strong." In *David Copperfield* (1850) the boy hero and narrator speaks of "going into the bar of a strange public-house for a glass of ale or porter." In *Great Expectations* (1861) Miss Havisham has inherited her wealth from her father, who had owned and operated a brewery.

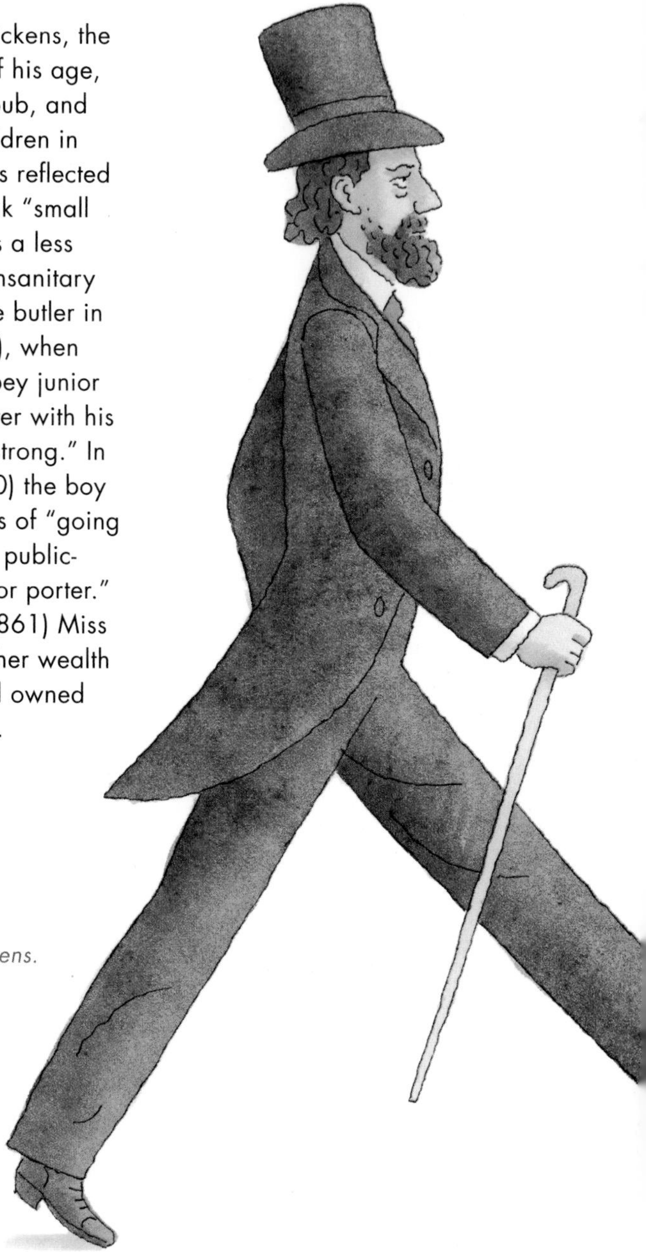

Charles Dickens.

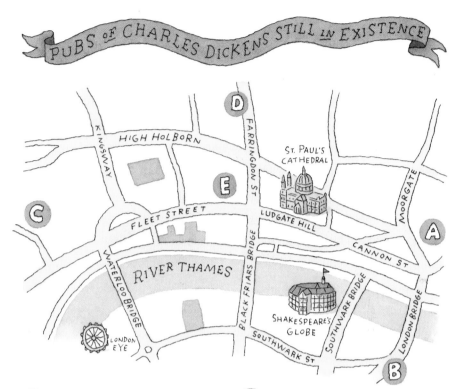

PUBS of CHARLES DICKENS STILL in EXISTENCE

Ⓐ George & Vulture

3 Castle Court
The quintessential Dickensian pub is mentioned frequently in *The Pickwick Papers* (1836–1837).

Ⓑ The George Inn

77 Borough High Street
Dickens often drank here and mentions it in Little Dorrit (1855–1857). His life insurance policy hangs on the wall.

Ⓒ Lamb & Flag

33 Rose Street
The pub bears a plaque commemorating Dickens's time as a regular.

Ⓓ One Tun

125/126 Saffron Hill
Located on the same street as Fagin's squalid lair in *Oliver Twist* (1839), the pub may have been the stand-in for Three Cripples public house of the novel as well. Dickens drank here in the 1830s.

Ⓔ Ye Olde Cheshire Cheese

145 Fleet Street
Dickens drank here as a young Fleet Street reporter.

Dust jacket of the Modern Library edition (1950).

DORCHESTER ALE

Thomas Hardy's beloved hometown of Dorchester, the setting for many of his novels, was renowned for its particularly strong ales. Hardy's appreciation for the beverage is evident in numerous passages from his work.

The Mayor of Casterbridge (1886) mentions a recipe (brew-speak dictionary required!) for the kind of home-brewed ale made in the country pubs of Hardy's Wessex:

15 pounds pale-ale malt (M & F from England)

2 pounds light brown sugar

Hops: Chinook for boil, circa 25 HBU

Fuggles for finish, circa 1 ounce 2 mins.

Chinook ⅛ dry hop

Fuggles ¼ dry hop

Mash: 15 quarts water

Mash in 130, raise to 158°F. Hold for 1½ hours.

Sparge with 30 quarts at 170°F. Add 1 teaspoon gypsum.

Boil about 6 hours. Add bittering hops 60 minutes before the end of the boil.

Wort should be 3.5–4 gallons gravity, gravity 1.30–1.145

Yeast: 1028 w yeast.

After 7 days, rack into 5 gallon carbouy and pitch champagne yeast.

Let ferment 4–6 days, then rack into 30 gallon carbouy.

If you don't have one, flush a 5 gallon with dry ice to remove oxygen.

Dry hop with hop bag for 2 weeks.

Remove hop bag, let sit an additional month.

Bottle: There may be a little carbonation. Add some champagne yeast when bottling.

Use corn sugar to prime: About ⅓ cup.

In 1968, Eldridge Pope Brewery in Dorchester, which first opened its doors in 1831, released a Thomas Hardy's Ale (at 11.7 percent alcohol by volume—the strongest beer produced in England at the time) to commemorate the fortieth anniversary of the British author's death. Printed on the label was Hardy's description of a strong Wessex ale from his novel *The Trumpet-Major* (1880): "It was the most beautiful colour that the eye of an artist in beer could desire; full in body, yet brisk as a volcano; piquant, yet without a twang; luminous as a autumn sunset; free from streakiness of taste; but, finally, rather heady."

Thomas Hardy.

THE TALL-TALE HEART

A poem known as "Lines on Ale" (1848) has been attributed, perhaps apocryphally, to Edgar Allan Poe. As the story goes, Poe wrote the poem at the Washington Tavern in Lowell, Massachusetts, to settle his bar tab, and the "original" copy hung on the wall of the tavern until about 1920. However, some scholars believe the tale to be a hoax foisted on the public by a mischievous bartender.

LINES ON ALE

Fill with mingled cream and amber,
I will drain that glass again.
Such hilarious visions clamber
Through the chamber of my brain—
Quaintest thoughts—queerest fancies
Come to life and fade away;
What care I how time advances?
I am drinking ale today.

STOUT FRIENDS

Herman Melville and Nathaniel Hawthorne.

Moby-Dick (1851) author Herman Melville clearly enjoyed the social bond among drinkers. Based on journal entries of both men starting in 1850, he and Nathaniel Hawthorne, of *The Scarlet Letter* (1850) fame, developed a convivial relationship over many drinking sessions.

In 1856 Melville visited Hawthorne, who was living in England after being appointed US consul in Liverpool. In a journal entry dated November 10, after traveling together by train to Southport, Melville wrote, "An agreeable day. Took a long walk by the sea. Sand & grass. Wild and desolate. A strong wind. Good talk. In the evening Stout & Fox & Geese." Fox & Goose was a local pub.

FOX & GOOSE

After exploring a cathedral in Chester on November 15, Hawthorne writes in his own journal that the two men "sat down in a small snuggery, behind the bar, and smoked cigars and drank some stout."

Stout, or porter, originated in London in the early 1700s. It's a dark beer typically made with unmalted barley roasted in a kiln.

THE BOOZE CRUSADER

H. L. Mencken, the caustic American journalist and social critic, was a staunch defender of alcohol during Prohibition, asserting that it was the drys, not the drinkers, who were the real savages. "Pithecanthropus erectus was a teetotaler, but the angels, you may be sure, know what is proper at 5 p.m."

H. L. Mencken.

He enjoyed all manner of alcoholic drinks, but beer was his passion, and Czech pilsner was his gold standard. At one point he made a pilgrimage to Pilsen, Czechoslovakia, declaring it "home of the best beer on earth and hence one of the great shrines of the human race."

Pilsner Urquell, introduced in 1842, is the original Czech pilsner.

HELP ME to keep Him PURE

PLEASE VOTE "AGAINST THE SALE OF LIQUORS"

1920s temperance poster.

GUINNESS IS GOOD FOR YOU

Since its beginnings in 1759, when a thirty-four-year-old Arthur Guinness signed a nine-thousand-year lease on a run-down property at St. James's Gate in Dublin, Guinness stout has remained one of the most iconic brews in all of beerdom. Forget the bottle or the can—Guinness on tap is the only way to drink it. Any well-versed beer drinker is familiar with the time-honored serving ritual. A proper pour means filling the pint glass two-thirds full. The bartender then walks off, allowing it to "surge and settle" for a few minutes, before returning to fill it the rest of the way. The customer drinks only when the line between the foamy head and the black beer has achieved peak contrast.

Statue of Arthur Guinness in his hometown of Celbridge in County Kildare.

James Joyce, whose own preference for wine has already been noted, called Guinness "the wine of the country" and made numerous references to the Guinness family and Ireland's national drink in his work.

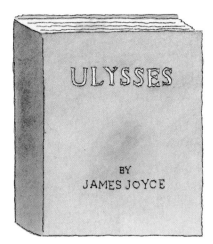

In *Ulysses* (1922) the Guinness brewery is a passing thought in the mind of Leopold Bloom: "Be interesting to get a pass through Hancock to see the brewery. Regular world in itself. Vats of porter, wonderful. Rats get in too. Drink themselves big as a collie floating. Dead drunk on the porter." Joyce also mentions the great-great-grandsons of Arthur, Lord Ardilaun and Lord Iveagh.

The unadorned first edition of the controversial novel published in 1922 by Sylvia Beach in Paris.

In *Finnegans Wake* (1939), "A Visit to Guinness' Brewery" is listed among the essay topics for the Earwicker children, Shem, Shaun, and Issy.

The St. James's Gate entrance to the Guinness Brewery.

Legend has it that Joyce submitted his own idea for an advertising slogan to the company—"Guinness—the free, the flow, the frothy freshener"—but like so many booze anecdotes, this story has been discredited. In a 2011

article in *James Joyce Quarterly*, Catherine Gubernatis Dannen concludes that the story was concocted for a 1982 Guinness advertisement to capitalize on the connection between the Guinness Company and the "Joyce Industry."

James Joyce.

Nonetheless, it's unlikely they would have replaced their already familiar slogan, "Guinness is good for you." In *Finnegans Wake*, Joyce writes, "Let us find that pint of porter place . . . Benjamin's Lea . . . and see the foamous homely brew, bebattled by bottle—then put James's Gate in my hand." He also puns on the famous slogan with the phrase "Genghis is ghoon for you."

Guinness poster, 1929.

THE BEER MILKSHAKE AND GOD'S VOICE

In John Steinbeck's 1945 novel *Cannery Row*, the main character, Doc, loves beer so much that somebody comments, "Someday [he'll] go in and order a beer milkshake."

John Steinbeck.

Doc obsesses about the idea and eventually gets up the nerve to order one, making up a recipe for the server on the spot. "Put in some milk, add half a bottle of beer. Give me the other half in a glass—no sugar in the milkshake." Steinbeck's bit of tomfoolery proved prescient—seventy years later, beer shakes could be found on chain-restaurant menus.

The American Pulitzer Prize–winning writer Anne Sexton, a pioneer of confessional poetry, favored martinis but enjoyed a beer with lunch. She opens her poem *"For Eleanor Boylan Talking with God"* (1962) with the line:

God has a brown voice,
as soft and full as beer.

MEN AND BEER

Nobody knows for sure what biological or social factors play into beer's overwhelmingly male appeal. Some taste scientists maintain that women have higher taste sensitivities and are less tolerant of bitterness. Society has also decreed that it's not "manly" to drink sweet and fruity "girly drinks." Strangely, Hemingway, the prototypical manly man, didn't pay much attention to beer. Going against type, he even enjoyed fruity cocktails like the daiquiri, albeit without the sugar.

A few beer-swilling alpha males:

In his 1947 crime novel *I, the Jury*, Mickey Spillane introduced the world to detective Mike Hammer. Among hard-boiled gumshoes, Hammer was an aberration—unlike his whiskey-swilling compatriots, he favored beer. In later novels Hammer drank Miller Lite (which Spillane just happened to be a pitchman for).

Mickey Spillane.

Norman Mailer, author of *The Naked and the Dead* (1948), describing his workday in a 1964 interview with *The Paris Review*, said, "In the afternoon, I usually needed a can of beer to prime me."

When times were lean, Charles Bukowski would default to beer. In 1988, *Life* magazine asked some noted scientists, theologians, artists, and authors to ponder the meaning of life. Bukowski's response:

> For those who believe in God, most of the bigger questions are answered. But for those of us who can't readily accept the God formula, the big answers don't remain stone-written. We adjust to new conditions and discoveries. We are pliable. Love need not be a command or faith a dictum. I am my own God. We are here to unlearn the teachings of the church, state and our education system. We are here to drink beer.

Charles Bukowski.

RUSSIAN HOPS

Russian poet and novelist Boris Pasternak, best known for *Doctor Zhivago* (1957), expressed obeisance to beer's distinguishing ingredient in his love poem "Hops" (1953):

> Beneath the willow wound round with ivy,
> We take cover from the worst
> Of the storm, with a greatcoat round
> Our shoulders and my hands around
> your waist.
>
> I've got it wrong. That isn't ivy
> Entwined in the bushes round
> The wood, but hops. You intoxicate me!
> Let's spread the greatcoat on the ground.
>
> —translated by Jon Stallworthy
> and Peter France

Boris Pasternak.

Stephen King.

ALL WORK AND NO BEER MAKES JACK A DULL BOY

The American master of horror and suspense Stephen King loved his suds but mostly drank at home. Now sober, he told *The Guardian* in 2013, "I didn't go out and drink in bars, because they were full of assholes like me."

He regards his most famous book, *The Shining* (1977), as a confession. The story, about a drunken father who wants to kill his own kid, grew out of his own feelings of antagonism toward his children when he was drinking. Writing the book was a way to get it out of his system.

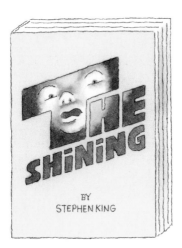

During King's drinking days, he revealed in *Writer's Digest,* "I like to write when I'm drunk. I've never had any particular problem writing that way, although I never wrote anything that was worth a dime while under the influence of pot or any of the hallucinogenics." In those days he considered drinking a boon to his craft: "Writers who drink constantly do not last long, but a writer who drinks carefully is probably a better writer," King has said.

The 1980 paperback edition featuring art from the Stanley Kubrick movie poster.

B IS FOR BEER

When American novelist Tom Robbins, author of *Even Cowgirls Get the Blues* (1976), saw a Frank Cotham cartoon in *The New Yorker* with the caption "I doubt that a children's book about beer would sell," he decided to take up the challenge.

The result was *B Is for Beer* (2009), which, in Robbins's own words, helped give kids "a clearer understanding of why their dad keeps a second refrigerator in the garage, and why he stays up late out there on school nights with his shirt off, listening to Aerosmith." The book undoubtedly appealed to adults as well and has gone on to sell a respectable 45,000 copies.

IN BEER WE TRUST

Today beer aficionados are luxuriating in a golden age of brewing. With increasingly complex and offbeat offerings, modern microbrewers continue to push the limits of what beer can be, moving it farther and farther away from the insipid lagers of yore. Among the quirky selections that an intrepid beer adventurer might encounter on modern liquor store shelves: avocado honey ale, pizza beer, doughnut chocolate peanut butter banana ale, coconut curry hefeweizen, bacon coffee porter, and oyster stout (as in bull testicles).

Beer snobs (previously an oxymoron) now have reason to rejoice. Modern brews have been quietly ascending to the rarified heights usually reserved for fine wine and whiskey. Cicerones, the beer equivalent of wine sommeliers, are now happy to pair your Buddha bowl with the perfect organic sour beer, and many restaurants now tout beer-tasting menus.

Venerated American sci-fi author Ray Bradbury was—true to form—ahead of his time when he summed up the beverage's highbrow/lowbrow appeal in his 1955 short story collection, The October Country, writing, "Beer's intellectual. What a shame so many idiots drink it."

A cicerone.

WHISKEY

Chapter 3

Bourbon does for me what the piece of cake did for Proust.
   —Walker Percy, *Esquire* (1975)

In drink lore few beverages can rival the colorful history or the pop-culture cachet of whiskey (aka whisky, bourbon, and scotch). The distilled spirit, made from grain mash, conjures images of feral Scottish Highlanders, grizzled western gunslingers, and hard-boiled detectives. Its literary bloodlines also run deep—the list of writers who have enjoyed the stuff is longer than any other spirit included in this volume.

THE WATER OF LIFE

The art of distillation, or the process of vaporizing and condensing a liquid to remove impurities and arrive at its essence, may have begun as early as 2000 BC in China, Egypt, or Mesopotamia. Over the millennia, distilling techniques spread to Europe, and somewhere between the eleventh and thirteenth centuries made their way to Scotland and Ireland via peripatetic monks. Scottish and Irish monasteries, lacking the proper climate for grape cultivation and wine production, turned to fermenting and distilling mash made from locally available grains, and whiskey was born. Scotland and Ireland still argue over who was first.

50

The Talisker Distillery on the Isle of Skye, Scotland, founded in 1830.

The term *whisky* derives from the Gaelic *uisge beatha*, meaning "water of life." The English modified it to *whiskybae*, and it was quickly shortened to *whisky*. *Whisky* is the spelling used in Scotland and Canada, and *whiskey* is used in Ireland and America.

THE TIPSY SCOTTISH BARDS

Scotch, as whisky from Scotland would come to be known, would soon be embraced as the country's national drink. Not surprisingly, it was consumed and adored by the country's national poet, Robert Burns. According to legend, he took his first sip of *uisge beatha* at the age of twenty-two in the coastal town of Irvine in North Ayrshire, where he had moved to learn the trade of flax combing.

Robert Burns.

A Scottish quaich, or traditional "friendship" drinking vessel, dating back to the sixteenth century and used by Highland clan chiefs to share whisky.

In his poem "Scotch Drink" (1785), Burns cites the spirit as inspiration:

O thou, my muse! Guid auld Scotch drink!
Whether thro' wimpling worms thou jink,
Or richly brown, ream owre the brink
In glorious faem,
Inspire me, till I lisp an' wink,
To sing thy name!

Sir Walter Scott.

Fellow Scotsman Sir Walter Scott, author of such classic novels as *Ivanhoe* (1820) and *Rob Roy* (1817), was equally enamored of his native drink. As Scotch whisky historian Iain Russell writes, Scott "saw good Scotch whisky as a noble drink and an integral part of the idealized Highland culture that provided the inspiration for much of his writing."

Scottish Highlander.

Scott's novel *Waverley* (1814), acknowledged as the first historical novel in the Western tradition, tells the story of a callow English soldier posted with his regiment to Scotland during the Jacobite uprising of 1745. There he is introduced to the heroic traditions, and whisky, of the Scottish Highlanders:

Peat-cutting spade—smoke from peat is often used during the malting process to enhance a Scotch whisky's character.

"The allowance of whisky, however, would have appeared prodigal to any but Highlanders, who, living entirely in the open air and in a very moist climate, can consume great quantities of ardent spirits without the usual baneful effects either upon the brain or constitution."

THE POWER AND THE GLORY OF SCOTCH

Twentieth-century writers across the pond were no less enthused by the drink of their ancestors.

Graham Greene, the preeminent British novelist, enjoyed J&B scotch whisky and soda. One of Greene's most famous, and controversial, characters is the nameless "whisky priest" in his novel *The Power and the Glory* (1940). Originally published in an edition of 3,500 copies, the book is generally regarded as his masterpiece. Set in Mexico in the 1930s, the novel depicts the priest ministering to his impoverished flock while under a haze of alcohol and fear brought on by government suppression of the Catholic Church.

One of literature's most famous drinking scenes occurs in Greene's *Our Man in Havana* (1958). The novel's protagonist, James Wormold—hapless vacuum cleaner salesman by day and master spy by night—engages an adversary in a game of checkers. He uses mini-bottles from his whiskey collection as game pieces—whiskey is on one side, bourbon on the other. "When you take a piece you drink it," Wormold explains. The whiskeys name-checked are Johnnie Walker Red, dimpled Haig, Cairgorm, and Grant's. The bourbons are Four Roses, Kentucky Tavern, Old Forester, and Old Taylor.

Graham Greene's favorite scotch.

Kingsley Amis's appreciation for all manner of spirits is well documented, yet he held a special place in his heart for scotch. In his paean to booze, *Every Day Drinking* (1983), he declares: "Scotch Whisky is my desert-island drink. I mean not only that it's my favorite, but that for me it comes nearer than anything else to being a drink for all occasions and all times of day, even with meals."

Kingsley Amis's Adler Universal 39 typewriter.

Amis, a prolific writer, was not averse to drinking while pecking away at the typewriter. In an interview with *The Paris Review* in 1975 he remarked, "So alcohol in moderate amounts and at a fairly leisurely speed is valuable to me—at least I think so. It could be that I could have written better without it . . . but it could also be true that I'd have written far less without it."

Relative to many of his sodden contemporaries, James Joyce was a lightweight, but nonetheless he enjoyed whiskey in addition the aforementioned wine and beer. Writing of Joyce's proclivity for only drinking at night, his biographer Richard Ellmann remarked, "He engaged in excess with considerable prudence."

A particularly Joycean anecdote: The writer, in failing health and stung by the underwhelming response to early drafts of *Finnegans Wake*, considered enlisting the aid of a coauthor in case he was unable to finish the novel himself. A prime candidate was James Stephens, not because he was best qualified but because the book cover could display their initials together—JJ&S—just like his favorite brand of Dublin whiskey—John Jameson & Son.

Brendan Behan, the Irish republican poet, novelist, and playwright, consumed vast quantities of Irish whiskey, and other libations, during his brief lifetime (he died from alcohol-related causes in 1964 at age forty-one). He was a self-described "drinker with a writing problem," and the subject of the Pogues' song "Streams of Whiskey."

James Joyce's preferred brand of whiskey.

THE WHISKEY DIASPORA IN AMERICA

DRINK, or DIE.

Many Scottish and Irish immigrants arrived in America during the seventeenth century to settle in the colonies, bringing their whiskey distillation know-how with them. Whiskey quickly became a valuable commodity and was used as currency during the American Revolutionary War.

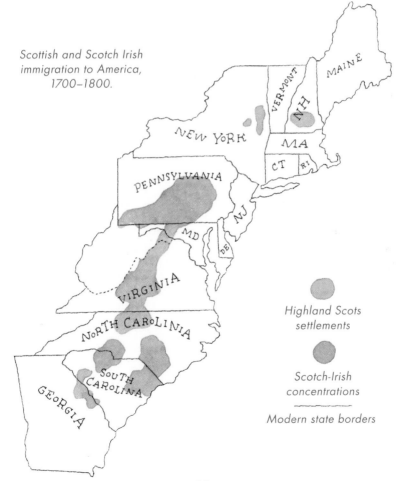

Scottish and Scotch Irish immigration to America, 1700–1800.

Highland Scots settlements

Scotch-Irish concentrations

Modern state borders

In 1791, Alexander Hamilton imposed a federal excise tax on whiskey to help pay down the Revolutionary War debt, prompting Scottish and Irish immigrant farmers in Pennsylvania to stage an uprising dubbed the Whiskey Rebellion. Tax collectors were attacked and in some cases whipped, tarred, and feathered. By 1794, the rebellion was quelled by government militia under orders from President George Washington. The tax remained until 1802, when it was repealed by President Thomas Jefferson.

During the Whiskey Rebellion, tax collectors were tarred and feathered by farmers and distillers.

SOUTHERN COMFORT

The most popular form of American whiskey is bourbon, and its birthplace is the American South. To be called bourbon, the spirit must be produced in the United States, aged in new oak charred barrels, and made from a grain mixture that includes at least 51 percent corn.

It's generally accepted that the name bourbon came from Bourbon County in upstate Kentucky in the nineteenth century. However, bourbon historian and author Michael Veach traces the moniker's origin to New Orleans and two men known as the Tarascon brothers. Arriving in Louisville around 1807 by way of the Cognac region of France, they began shipping local whiskey down the Ohio River to Louisiana's port city. Demand grew for "that whiskey they sell on Bourbon Street," which eventually became "that bourbon whiskey."

Barrel charring breaks down the oak's hemicellulose into sugars that are then caramelized, imparting to bourbon its distinctive flavor.

Corn whiskey, a variation made from a mash of at least 80 percent corn, was enjoyed and celebrated by the American poet, playwright, and novelist Langston Hughes, born in Joplin, Missouri. His "Hey-Hey Blues" appeared in the pages of *The New Yorker* in 1939:

Langston Hughes.

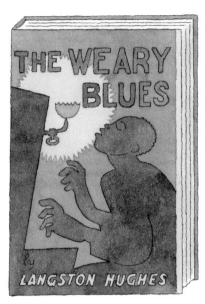

Cause I can HEY on water,
I said HEY-HEY on beer,
HEY on water,
And HEY-HEY on beer,
But gimme good corn whiskey
And I'll HEY-HEY-HEY—and cheer!

Hughes's debut poetry collection was published in 1926, during Prohibition, when he was twenty-four years old.

More than a few other southern scribes partook of the local hooch, including Louisiana novelist Walker Percy, author of *The Moviegoer* (1961). He appreciated the aesthetic of bourbon drinking, particularly knocking it back neat. In an article he wrote for *Esquire* in 1975, simply titled "Bourbon," Walker praised the use of the spirit to "warm the heart, to reduce the anomie of the late twentieth century, to cure the cold phlegm of Wednesday afternoons."

Walker Percy.

WHISKEY'S POET LAUREATE

William Faulkner, the southerner and celebrated Nobel laureate who declared, "Civilization begins with distillation," was in a league of his own, and may have been whiskey's greatest literary champion.

William Faulkner.

Born in New Albany, Mississippi, on September 25, 1897, Faulkner grew up in Oxford and would remain in the region, the fictional Yoknapatawpha County, where all of his novels were set, for most of his life.

Faulkner's relationship to drink began in 1918, when his high school sweetheart, Estelle Oldham, married another man. Faulkner was heartbroken and turned to the bottle. He relocated briefly to New Haven, Connecticut, to stay with Philip Stone, a family friend and Yale graduate, who would become the young writer's mentor, introducing him to the work of James Joyce, Ezra Pound, and T. S. Eliot.

Faulkner attended the University of Mississippi ("Ole Miss") for just three semesters, receiving a D in English, before dropping out. During this period he was reportedly downing a quart of bourbon a day. Seven years later, in 1926, he published his first novel, *Soldier's Pay*, which was well received. It contains the line "What can equal a mother's love? Except a good drink of whiskey."

Colonel Reb, Ole Miss's controversial mascot, was retired in 2003.

In 1929 he learned that Estelle was divorcing after ten years of marriage, and she and Faulkner were married two months later, in June.

Later that same year his first major novel, *The Sound and the Fury*, was published. The jigsaw puzzle narrative and post-Joycean stream-of-consciousness technique made for difficult reading, but the book would later be hailed as a masterpiece.

Estelle Oldham.

In 1930, as Faulkner continued to drink heavily, his second acclaimed novel, *As I Lay Dying*, was published. Faulkner readily admitted to drinking while he worked. As he would later explain to his French translator, Maurice Edgar Coindreau: "You see, I usually write at night. I always keep my whiskey within reach; so many ideas that I can't remember in the morning pop into my head."

1929 first edition published by Jonathan Cape & Harrison Smith.

Hemingway, known for his disciplined separation of work and drink, once said of Faulkner, "I can tell right in the middle of the page when he's had his first one."

One of the central characters in *Light in August*, Faulkner's epic 1932 novel set in the American South during Prohibition, was a whiskey bootlegger named Joe Christmas. In this passage Faulkner eloquently describes the act of drinking whiskey: "The whiskey went down his throat cold as molasses. . . . Then the whiskey began to burn in him . . . while thinking became one with the slow, hot coiling and recoiling of his entrails."

Metro Goldwyn Mayer

GRATIA ARTIS

TRADE   MARK

That same year, to help pay the bills, Faulkner headed to Hollywood to work part-time as a screenwriter for MGM—a dalliance with Tinseltown that would continue for decades.

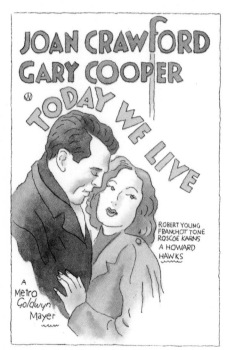

JOAN CRAWFORD
GARY COOPER
TODAY WE LIVE

ROBERT YOUNG
FRANCHOT TONE
ROSCOE KARNS
A HOWARD
HAWKS

A
Metro
Goldwyn
Mayer

Original one-sheet movie poster.

In an interview the director Howard Hawks recalled meeting the writer over a "couple quarts of whiskey" to discuss writing the screenplay that would become *Today We Live*, a 1933 hit movie starring Gary Cooper and Joan Crawford. Other screen credits would include *To Have and Have Not* (1944) and *The Big Sleep* (1946).

During his increasingly frequent forays to Hollywood, Faulkner's favorite hangout was the Musso & Frank Grill, where he was known to order Old Grand-Dad bourbon.

In 1936, *Absalom, Absalom!* was published, today widely regarded as his greatest novel. While visiting the Algonquin Hotel in New York City in 1937, a sozzled Faulkner passed out against a steam radiator, severely burning his back. When asked about his work, he would say, "Hell, how do I know what it means? I was drunk when I wrote it."

In 1950, Faulkner received the Nobel Prize in Literature. Five years later he would receive the Pulitzer Prize and the National Book Award for his novel *A Fable*. By then, his bourbon consumption was rationalized as "treatment" for his various maladies, including sore throats, a bad back, and general malaise.

One of Bill's many bourbons.

A Faulkner tobacco pipe manufactured by Digby of London.

The Algonquin incident.

In 1962 he was awarded a second Pulitzer Prize for his novel *The Reivers*, only to die of a heart attack a month later at the age of sixty-four. A fitting epitaph would have been his prescription for a successful day of work: "The tools that I need for my trade are simply pen, paper, food, tobacco, and a little whiskey."

THE MINT JULEP

William Faulkner certainly enjoyed whiskey straight (Jack Daniel's and Old Crow were favorites), and a toddy—hot or cold—was a frequent companion, but his signature drink was the mint julep.

The word *julep* derives from the ancient Persian *gulab,* a rose-petal-flavored water (more commonly known in the West today as rosewater) still used in food, drinks, perfume, cosmetics, and religious ceremonies. In the Mediterranean, indigenous mint replaced the rose petals, and the drink eventually made its way to the New World, where, in the American South, it was combined with bourbon.

Since 1938, the cocktail has been a prominent feature of the Kentucky Derby, and in 1983 it became the horse race's official drink. Each year, roughly 120,000 juleps are served at the race over the course of two days.

Faulkner loved the drink so much that he had his own simple recipe for it, displayed on a typewritten notecard at his Rowan Oak estate in Oxford, Mississippi: whiskey, 1 tsp sugar, ice, mint served in a metal cup. A more precise version follows:

Faulkner's Mint Julep

Leaves from 4 to 5 mint sprigs, plus sprig for garnish

1 tablespoon sugar

2 teaspoons water

Crushed ice

2½ ounces bourbon

In a metal julep cup or highball glass, gently muddle mint leaves after removing stems. Add sugar and water and fill with crushed ice. Add bourbon and garnish with a mint sprig.

A REAL-LIFE JAY GATSBY

During Prohibition, one of America's most notorious whiskey bootleggers was George Remus, known for his peculiar habit of referring to himself in the third person. Remus, a Midwest criminal defense lawyer, scoured the Volstead Act looking for loopholes that would enable him to buy and sell stockpiles of bonded whiskey (government-licensed "medicinal" whiskey available with a doctor's prescription). He discovered that by owning distilleries and wholesale drug companies, he could legally buy and sell large quantities of alcohol and then divert them for illegal sale.

With organized crime controlling most of Chicago, Remus moved to Cincinnati, where 80 percent of America's bonded whiskey was located. He quickly became enormously wealthy but was eventually caught and convicted in 1921. "The King of the Bootleggers" may have been an inspiration for Jay Gatsby, the title character in F. Scott Fitzgerald's novel *The Great Gatsby* (1925). Fitzgerald purportedly met him by chance at a hotel in Louisville and was captivated by his larger-than-life personality.

George Remus.

WHISKEY SOUR

In 1925 in France, Ernest Hemingway, a fledgling writer who had yet to write his first novel, met F. Scott Fitzgerald, an established literary star three years his senior. In his Parisian memoir, *A Moveable Feast* (1964), Hemingway recounts an episode involving whiskey sours. Fitzgerald, feeling unwell, is convinced he's catching "congestion of the lungs," or pneumonia. An exasperated Hemingway tries to calm him down: "'Look, Scott,'" I said, "'You're perfectly O.K. If you want to do the best thing to keep from catching cold, just stay in bed and I'll order us each a lemonade and whisky.'"

He summons a waiter and orders two *citron pressés* (pressed lemon juice) and two double whiskeys. Fitzgerald is soon feeling better. They proceed to drink two more rounds before Fitzgerald passes out and is carted off to bed.

In his description, Hemingway, never fond of sweet drinks, omits the sweetener typically included in the cocktail's ingredients to offset the bitterness of the lemon.

Traditional Whiskey Sour

2 ounces whiskey (bourbon)

⅔ ounce freshly squeezed lemon juice

1 teaspoon superfine sugar (or ¾ ounce simple syrup)

1 egg white (optional)

Cracked ice

Maraschino cherry or lemon wedge for garnish

Shake the whiskey, juice, sugar, and egg white (if using), well with cracked ice. Strain into a chilled cocktail glass. Garnish with a maraschino cherry or lemon wedge.

HARD-BOILED AND THREE SHEETS TO THE WIND

The Maltese Falcon.

Raymond Chandler and Dashiell Hammett were two whiskey-loving founders of the so-called hard-boiled school of detective fiction. Chandler's archetypal character Philip Marlowe, a private detective who appeared in many of his stories, always kept a bottle of Old Forester in his office. Chandler once said, "There is no bad whiskey. There are only some whiskeys that aren't as good as others." Dashiell Hammett's most famous detective character, Sam Spade, was also a whiskey man. In *The Maltese Falcon* (1930), he drinks a Manhattan cocktail (whiskey, sweet vermouth, and bitters) from a cup. Hammett's fifth and final detective novel, *The Thin Man* (1934), was published only months after the repeal of Prohibition. It was eagerly embraced by a public ready to drink, and scotch perfumes its pages from beginning to end.

For thirty years American dramatist, screenwriter, and polemicist Lillian Hellman maintained a tumultuous on-and-off relationship with Hammett. On the strength of two successful plays she wrote in the 1930s, *The Children's Hour* (1934) and *The Little Foxes* (1939), Hellman became the first woman to gain access into the exclusive all-male club of American playwrights.

Lillian Hellman.

Dorothy Parker.

And she was no slouch as a boozer—she enjoyed drinking scotch neat out of a wineglass. Whiskey was typically considered a man's drink, but Hellman was one of several notable exceptions. As was her longtime friend Dorothy Parker, who settled on scotch as her drink of choice after flirtations with gin martinis and champagne.

PANDORA IN BLUE JEANS

In the mid-1950s an unknown, bedraggled housewife from New Hampshire with a penchant for whiskey would shock the American public with her debut novel, which became an explosive best seller and one of the most controversial novels of the twentieth century. It would spawn a movie and a long-running television soap opera. It was *Peyton Place* by Grace Metalious. Metalious would become wealthy and famous overnight, as well as an unwitting feminist trailblazer, inspiring women all over America who were chafing under the restrictive social norms of the Eisenhower era.

Born into poverty on September 8, 1924, in the mill town of Manchester, New Hampshire, as Marie Grace DeRepentigny, Metalious was of French Canadian ancestry. She was raised in a ramshackle cottage near the Merrimack River, the same river that flowed south through Lowell, Massachusetts, the hometown of French Canadian Jack Kerouac.

Grace Metalious.

66

Metalious's parents separated when she was eleven, and words were her refuge from a troubled home. At eighteen, despite dreaming of a different life for herself, she married her high school sweetheart, George Metalious, and settled into her presumptive roles as homemaker and mother-to-be.

The couple later settled in Gilmanton, New Hampshire, where George had been offered a position as a school principal, eventually having three children. Metalious focused seriously on her writing, often working up to fourteen hours a day while shirking her domestic responsibilities.

Her writing area was always immaculate, but the rest of the house was a pigsty, and her children were often neglected.

Metalious was the antithesis of the demure New England housewife: she smoked, drank whiskey, used salty language, and wore baggy flannel shirts and jeans, all of which drew sidelong glances from her incredulous neighbors. She drank to deal with her emotional isolation. Her favorite watering hole was the Tavern Hotel in the nearby town of Laconia (a model for Peyton Place), where she enjoyed Canadian Club whiskey with ginger ale and a lemon twist.

By the spring of 1955, Metalious had the first draft of a manuscript, with the working title *The Tree and the Blossom*, but it was rejected by all the major publishers for its racy content. It eventually landed on the desk of Kitty Messner, the president of Julian Messner, Inc. Messner loved everything about the book except the title and wanted it changed to the name of the town where the novel was set—Peyton Place. At age thirty-two, Metalious had a book deal. The novel, published in 1956, was an instant sensation and turned her into a celebrity overnight. It chronicled the dark secrets and sinister machinations lurking beneath the placid surface of a seemingly respectable New England town. Its lurid depictions of sex, rape, public drunkenness, murder, incest, abortion, and suicide imperiled the Norman Rockwell–like image of 1950s New England.

1956 first edition published by Messner.

Critical reviews were mostly negative, with one notable exception—the *New York Times Book Review* praised *Peyton Place* for taking a stand "against the false fronts and bourgeois pretensions of allegedly respectable communities." To cope with the pressures of her newfound fame and notoriety, Metalious started plowing through multiple packs of unfiltered Parliaments a day and drinking heavily.

Grace's 1951 white Cadillac convertible.

For the inhabitants of Gilmanton, the novel struck too close to home. Grace was threatened with libel lawsuits, her kids were harassed, and George lost his job. Her marriage soon cracked under the pressure. The scandalous book was condemned by sanctimonious politicians and denounced from the pulpit. Metalious defended herself: "To talk about adults without talking about their sex drives is like talking about a window without glass."

The remaining seven years of Grace's short life would be a whirlwind of lavish spending, Hollywood parties, numerous affairs, and copious amounts of whiskey. Having gone through most of her money, Grace went on to grind out three more novels before succumbing to cirrhosis of the liver at age thirty-nine. Toward the end, doctors believed she had been drinking a fifth of whiskey every day.

Peyton Place remained on the *New York Times* best-seller list for fifty-nine weeks, making it the top-selling novel of the twentieth century, just ahead of Margaret Mitchell's *Gone with the Wind* (1936).

SCOTCH VERSUS BOURBON:
THE YANKEE WHISKEY CONNOISSEUR

Mark Twain.

The American writer, adventurer, and irascible humorist Samuel Langhorne Clemens, better known by his nom de plume, Mark Twain, was a devotee of his native spirit, American bourbon (Old Crow being his favorite)—until he discovered scotch whisky.

During a trip across the Atlantic to England in 1873, he was introduced to a scotch and lemon juice cocktail. Captivated by the beverage, he wrote home to his wife, Livy, from the Langham Hotel in London: "Livy my darling, I want you to be sure & remember to have in the bathroom, when I arrive, a bottle of Scotch whisky, a lemon, some crushed sugar, and a bottle of Angostura bitters."

The beloved author of *The Adventures of Tom Sawyer* (1876) would eventually start drinking his scotch neat, enjoying it in tandem with his pipe or cigars, and calling it "my pet of all brews."

HITTING THE BOTTLE WITH GENE, NORM, AND MR. GONZO

The prolific playwright Eugene O'Neill is exhibit A for the case that writing and drinking, though not necessarily at the same time, enhance productivity. Anointed "America's Shakespeare," he drank whiskey like a fish—and produced sixteen new plays in his first decade of writing professionally. Along the way he managed to land on the cover of *Time* and collect a Nobel Prize in Literature and three Pulitzers.

O'Neill on the cover of Time *magazine, February 13, 1928.*

He wrote what he knew—his work is filled with alcoholic lowlifes. In *The Iceman Cometh* (1939), his whiskey-swilling alter ego, Jimmy, professes, "I discovered early in life that living frightened me when I was sober."

Norman Mailer.

The pugnacious novelist Norman Mailer had little to say on the subject of alcohol when queried about it, but his reputation as an inveterate boozer was well known. He enjoyed bourbon but *never* scotch: "I'm an American writer, I drink bourbon, an American drink. . . . That's the difference between a great writer and someone who'll never be a great writer—someone who knows the difference between Scotch and bourbon."

Hunter S. Thompson.

For Hunter S. Thompson, the "gonzo journalist" and author of *Fear and Loathing in Las Vegas* (1972), mind alteration was a way of life—booze, marijuana, LSD, amyl nitrite, cocaine, ether, and mescaline all found their way into his system. But like Twain, he had a deep appreciation for both bourbon and scotch—Wild Turkey to write and Chivas Regal scotch to read the morning papers. He called Chivas on the rocks his "snow cone." Thompson's advice for fledgling party animals: "Sleep late, have fun, get wild, drink whiskey and drive fast on empty streets with nothing in mind but falling in love and not getting arrested. . . . *Res ipsa loquitur.* Let the good times roll."

THE MOST COMPLEX SPIRIT ON EARTH

Throughout recorded history, whiskey has remained a hard-liquor stalwart, impervious to fluctuating booze fashions. For drinkers who prefer their liquor neat, the clear spirits—vodka and gin—simply can't compete with a premium whiskey's Technicolor assault on the nose and tongue. Unlike whiskey, vodka and gin don't age, a necessary precondition for olfactory and taste bud nirvana.

The quality and breadth of whiskey offerings available today is mind-boggling. The traditional whiskey-producing countries no longer have an exclusive claim to the title "best in the world." It's difficult to imagine what Robert Burns would have made of modern Japanese single-malts that consistently beat those from Scotland in blind taste tests.

George Bernard Shaw, who wasn't actually much of a drinker, may have summed up the spirit's universal appeal best when he declared, "Whiskey is liquid sunshine."

GIN

Chapter 4

Juniper
berry.

One martini is all right, two is too many, three is not enough.
—James Thurber, *Time* magazine (1960)

Gin has probably sparked more literary inspiration than any liquid distillate other than whiskey, but it wasn't always the respectable, civilized spirit that it is today. Social critics in eighteenth-century Georgian England regarded it as a plague on society—the crack cocaine of its day. In the early nineteenth century the advent of cocktails, or "mixed drinks," in London helped rehabilitate gin's lowly reputation.

In America, Prohibition paradoxically helped spur the Roaring Twenties—the sodden era of flappers, jazz, and art deco that followed World War I. It was a glamorous decade, when the writing life and the drinking life merged powerfully, ushering in a golden age of hard-drinking men and women of letters. Gin would be a big part of it.

DUTCH COURAGE

Gin derives its distinctive piney scent and flavor from *Juniperus communis*, also known as the juniper berry.

The spirit's murky origins can be traced back to the sixteenth-century lowlands of Belgium and Holland. Genever, the Dutch ancestor to modern gin, was initially sold in chemist shops for its medicinal properties. It was used to treat a host of ailments, including gout and gallstones.

British troops fighting in the Thirty Years' War (1618–1648) were given Dutch gin to warm their bodies in the cold weather and to calm their nerves before battle. The soldiers dubbed it "Dutch courage."

William of Orange, ruler of the Dutch Republic, did much to popularize the spirit in England during his occupation of the British throne starting in 1689. During his reign he boycotted imports of brandy, a popular fortified wine from archenemy France. This opened the floodgates for Dutch distillers, who were soon shipping boatloads of genever to England as quickly as they could produce it.

Plague doctors in the seventeenth century wore beak masks (the origin of the term quack) filled with crushed juniper berries, believed to protect against the epidemic.

THE LONDON GIN CRAZE

Gin, inexpensive to produce and safer to drink than London's pathogen-laced water, became all the rage in Britain during the early eighteenth century, a period known as the Gin Craze. At one point there was one gin distillery for every four houses.

To curb consumption, a series of reforms were enacted, starting with the Gin Act of 1736, which led to rioting in the streets and resulted in reputable sellers going out of business. Bootleggers thrived, often selling gin of dubious quality—sometimes flavored with turpentine rather than juniper—with colorful names such as Ladies' Delight and Cuckold's Comfort.

The popularity of gin among the poor contributed to its growing unsavory reputation. Dubbed "Mother's ruin," the spirit's deleterious effect on the lower classes was famously depicted in William Hogarth's satirical engraving *Gin Lane* (1751), sparking public outcry and further reform.

The emergence of the cocktail, or mixed drink, at the end of the eighteenth century in London helped to restore gin's status over time, and by 1823, the hot gin twist—hot water and gin with sugar and lemon juice—was the city's most popular drink.

Old Tom, the most popular gin style of the nineteenth century, was a bridge between the early sweet Dutch genever and later London dry styles.

Charles Dickens was a temperate drinker whose own cellar contained brandy, rum, whiskey, wine, and gin. His great-grandson, Cedric Dickens, writes in *Drinking with Dickens* (1998) that the famed author "loved the ritual of mixing the evening glass of Gin Punch, which he performed with all the energy and discrimination of Mr. Micawber"—a reference to the gin-punch-drinking character from *David Copperfield* (1850).

THE VENERABLE G & T

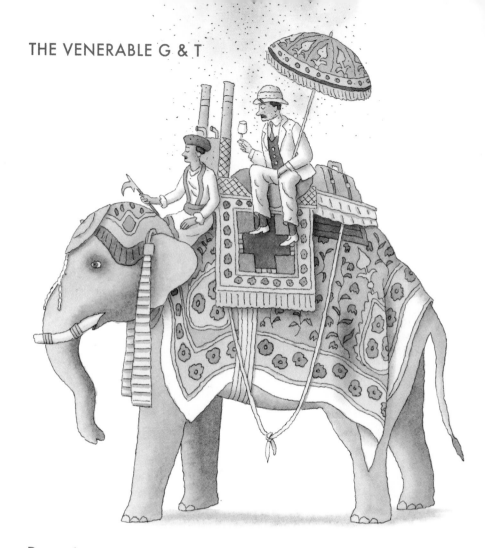

During the 1800s, the gin and tonic became the favorite drink of the army of the British East India Company. Troops stationed in India had been urged to ingest a daily dose of quinine, a powder ground from the bark of the cinchona tree, as a protective measure against malaria. Seeking to counter the bitterness of the quinine powder, officers began dissolving the substance in a mixture of sugar, carbonated water, and lime. It was only a matter of time before the concoction was combined with the typical soldier's daily shots of gin, and the gin and tonic was born.

Strangely, the actual term "gin and tonic" doesn't seem to turn up in fiction until P. G. Wodehouse's *Right Ho, Jeeves*, in 1922.

To this day, the gin and tonic remains a foundational piece of the gin cocktail canon. Contemporary British novelist Lawrence Osborne describes the classic drink in his trenchant travelogue on alcohol and Islam, *The Wet and the Dry* (2013): "The drink comes with a dim music of ice cubes and a perfume that touches the nose like a smell of warmed grass. Ease returns. It's like cold steel in liquid form."

Jeeves.

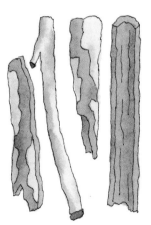

Cinchona bark, the source of quinine.

American writer John Cheever, "the Chekhov of the Suburbs," was another heavy imbiber of the gin and tonic, referring to Gilbey's gin as "mother's milk." He wrote a self-reflective short story that appeared in *The New Yorker* in 1953, entitled "The Sorrows of Gin," about a little girl affected by the drinking and partying of her parents.

Cheever's "mother milk."

THE LUBRICATED LIBRARIAN

There may have been no more ardent G & T enthusiast among the literary set than Philip Larkin, the bespectacled British poet from Coventry, England. In 2001, Larkin's longtime lover Monica Jones died, leaving behind some fourteen hundred letters from Larkin (who had died in 1985). The missives, compiled and edited by Anthony Thwaite under the title *Letters to Monica,* were published in 2010. Besides offering a glimpse into the mind of a famously inscrutable writer, they also confirm his affinity for gin and tonic.

Larkin was the stereotypical fussy and repressed Englishman, whose quasi-reclusive lifestyle has been well documented. A self-styled wallower in misery, he once said, "Deprivation is for me what daffodils were for Wordsworth," and he described himself as "an egg sculpted in lard, with goggles on."

Philip Larkin.

Larkin attended Oxford in the early 1940s. There he befriended Kingsley Amis, the two bonding over shared middle-class backgrounds, enthusiasm for jazz, distaste for English modernist writers, and a penchant for booze. They invented a game called "horsepissing" in which they amused themselves endlessly by replacing key words in famous works of literature with obscenities.

80

The friendship would later become frayed after the publication of Amis's novel *Lucky Jim* in 1954. Although the book was dedicated to Larkin, it contained some transparent references to his relationship with Monica Jones that rankled the poet.

Kingsley Amis.

Larkin was notoriously ambivalent about his relationships with women, and he clung to the notion that his aversion to intimacy was a necessary condition for his art. He once wrote in his diary that "sex is too good to share with anyone else." Nonetheless, at one point he managed to find himself juggling affairs with three different women, including Jones. In spite of his occasional dalliances over the years, she would stick with him.

Monica Jones.

Larkin first met Jones at University College of Leicester in 1946, when they were both twenty-four. He was an assistant librarian, and she was a lecturer in the English department. In addition to the two sharing intellectual pursuits, Jones matched Larkin's enthusiasm for gin and tonics—at home she enjoyed them served in goblets the size of small fishbowls.

Larkin moved to Ireland in 1950 after being appointed sub-librarian at the Queen's University of Belfast, marking the beginning of their written correspondence. They had become lovers by then, and their relationship would last more than forty years, until the poet's death.

Larkin often addressed Monica as his "dearest bun" in his letters, a nod to Beatrix Potter's bunnies, whom they both shared a fondness for. References to gin and drinking are also scattered throughout:

PHILIP LARKIN
Letters to Monica

First edition, Faber & Faber, London, 2010.

> On Friday I "got drunk"—
> this is perhaps a theatrical way
> of saying I had two gins before
> supper instead of one.

> I can feel my mind digging up years-old slights and getting furious over them. Only drink releases me from this bondage. I'm not the sort that gets angry when drunk.

> God. Hay fever & drink. Still can't quite taste gin, but am certainly feeling drunk. How did you think the poems looked? I like them drunk, prefer *Posterity* sober.

Larkin's wicker rabbit, a gift from Monica.

He also expressed existential angst over the seeming pointlessness of his labors:

> *Morning, noon & bloody night,*
> *Seven sodding days a week,*
> *I slave at filthy work, that might*
> *Be done by any book-drunk freak.*
> *This goes on till I kick the bucket:*
> *FUCK IT FUCK IT FUCK IT FUCK IT.*

Later in life he would start drinking as soon as he returned home from his job running the Hull University library. He enjoyed solitary nights drinking and listening to his beloved jazz records. In a footnote to the second edition of *All What Jazz* (1985), a compilation of record reviews he wrote for the *Daily Telegraph*, he states: "Listening to new jazz records for an hour with a pint of gin and tonic is the best remedy for a day's work I know."

Larkin's jazz favorites were prebop icons like Louis Armstrong, Duke Ellington, and Sidney Bechet.

In his poem "Sympathy in White Major" (1974) he actually sets down in verse the instructions for making a perfect gin and tonic:

When I drop four cubes of ice
Chimingly in a glass, and add
Three goes of gin, a lemon slice,
And let a ten-ounce tonic void
In foaming gulps until it smothers
Everything else up to the edge . . .

Larkin always feared that he would die at sixty-three like his father—and he did. Delivering the eulogy, Kingsley Amis summed him up as a private man "who found the universe a bleak and hostile place and recognized clearly the disagreeable realities of human life, above all the dreadful effects of time on all we have and are."

THE LIQUID FUEL OF THE ROARING TWENTIES

Prohibition in the United States (1920–1933) sent gin production underground. The spirit's ease of production—unlike whiskey, it was ready to drink right away—made it popular with bootleggers. It became the most common liquor offered at the illicit drinking establishments known as speakeasies.

Heightened demand for the spirit spawned the creation of "bathtub gin," produced in private homes for consumption in hidden back rooms as well as speakeasies. Gin required water, and the large jugs used to steep the ingredients were too big to fit under a sink tap, so a bathtub tap was used.

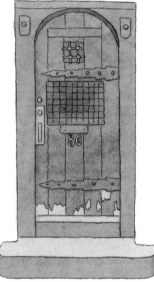

Life magazine cover art by John Held Jr., February 18, 1926.

The unmarked door of Chumley's, an original New York City speakeasy at 86 Bedford Street. Established in 1922 and still open today, it catered to a literary set that included F. Scott Fitzgerald, Willa Cather, William Faulkner, Ring Lardner, John Dos Passos, Theodore Dreiser, and later the Beat Generation.

Unscrupulous producers turned to widely available, and toxic, industrial alcohols like methanol (used in fuels, polishes, and lubricants) as a substitute for ethanol (the grain alcohol and basic intoxicating agent in all spirits). This contributed to bathtub gin's dubious reputation—ten thousand people died from drinking bad gin and other poisonous spirits during Prohibition.

In the 1910s and '20s the Bronx cocktail was a popular drink made with gin, sweet and dry vermouth, and orange juice. It was the kissing cousin of the equally popular rye-whiskey-based Manhattan cocktail. According to sociologist, historian, civil rights activist, and author W. E. B. Du Bois, knowing the difference between the two drinks signaled one's drinkerly erudition and socioeconomic status. In his 1940 autobiographical work *Dusk of Dawn*, Du Bois describes a Brooks Brothers–clad white minister who "plays keen golf, smokes a rare weed and knows a Bronx cocktail from a Manhattan."

THE ORIGINAL GREENWICH VILLAGE BOHEMIAN

Gin-loving American poet Maxwell Bodenheim may have been the spirit's first Jazz Age casualty. He arrived in New York in 1915, quickly achieving a measure of critical success and appearing in poetry journals alongside Ezra Pound and Edgar Lee Masters. He was soon garnering a reputation as a dissolute and lecherous ladies' man. His friend Ben Hecht wrote that Max was "kicked down more flights of stairs than any poet of whom I have heard or read."

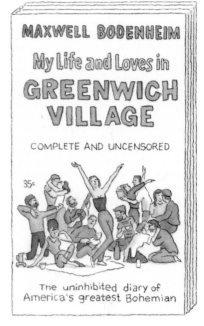

Paperback edition published by Belmont, 1961.

His early success was followed by a period of rapid decline. By the end of his life, he was spending hours in his favorite booth at the San Remo Café on MacDougal Street, peddling his poems in exchange for money to buy gin.

Maxwell Bodenheim.

His final, posthumously published book, *My Life and Loves in Greenwich Village* (1954), was a ghostwritten volume cobbled together from his drunken ramblings.

THE SHIT-FACED PRODIGY OF THE JAZZ AGE

F. Scott Fitzgerald did his part to help glamorize gin. The celebrated American writer, along with his flapper wife, Zelda, encapsulated and chronicled the spirit and excesses of the era. His premature death at age forty-four was the culmination of years of hard drinking.

At the time of his graduation from Princeton in 1916, his immoderate drinking patterns were already well established. Following the 1920 publication of his wildly successful debut novel, *This Side of Paradise*, Fitzgerald soon acquired a reputation as a boorish cocktail-party drunk, known for hurling ashtrays and insults.

Ernest Hemingway would later refer to him as a lightweight in *A Moveable Feast*, writing that "it was hard to accept him as a drunkard, since he was affected by such small quantities of alcohol."

F. Scott Fitzgerald.

The gin rickey—gin, ice, club soda, and half a squeezed lime—was the most popular gin drink of the late nineteenth and early twentieth centuries and a favorite of Fitzgerald's. In a scene from *The Great Gatsby* (1925), the cocktail makes an appearance in a hotel room on a stiflingly hot day:

> Tom came back, preceding four gin rickeys that clicked full of ice.
> Gatsby took up his drink.
> "They certainly look cool," he said, with visible tension.
> We drank in long, greedy swallows.

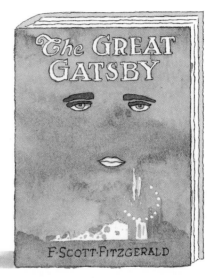

First edition published by Scribner's, 1925. Fitzgerald, inspired by the lavish parties he attended on Long Island, began planning the novel in 1923.

Upon its initial publication in 1925, *Gatsby* was considered a flop, receiving mixed reviews and selling just over twenty thousand copies. Although it was never popular in Fitzgerald's lifetime, today it is among the most beloved of American novels and continues to sell more than five hundred thousand copies a year.

Zelda Fitzgerald.

However, many of Fitzgerald's contemporaries saw it for the masterpiece that it was. In a letter to Fitzgerald, T. S. Eliot wrote, "It seems to me to be the first step that American fiction has taken since Henry James."

Fitzgerald, whose preferred gin was said to be Gordon's, credited alcohol with fueling his creative process. He wrote: "Drink heightens feeling. When I drink, it heightens my emotions and I put it in a story. . . . My stories when written sober are stupid."

But the cumulative effect of years of intemperance eventually took a toll. Between 1933 and 1937, Scott was hospitalized for alcoholism eight times.

Following a series of career setbacks, Fitzgerald moved to Los Angeles in 1937 to work as a screenwriter for the film studio MGM. By this time, he needed to earn money to support Zelda, who was in a sanitarium, and his daughter, Scottie, a student at Vassar. Fitzgerald's secretary and assistant in LA, Frances Kroll Ring, wrote in her memoir of stuffing empty gin bottles into burlap potato sacks and disposing of them in a brushy ravine.

Early twentieth-century
Gordon's gin label.

SCREEN WRITERS' GUILD INC.

Membership Card
ACTIVE

F. SCOTT FITZGERALD
Member

Issued SEP 23 1938 193___

Fitzgerald died of a heart attack on December 21, 1940, at his mistress's Hollywood apartment. His unfinished novel, *The Last Tycoon,* was published posthumously in 1941.

HOLLYWOODLAND

Joan Didion.

THE VERSATILE MIXER

Unlike whiskey or tequila, gin is seldom drunk neat. Most literary enthusiasts of the spirit preferred it in the form of one of its iconic cocktail iterations, such as Larkin's aforementioned gin and tonic, or, in the case of Joan Didion, adulterated with hot water. The author described her remedy for writer's block in the preface to *Slouching Towards Bethlehem* (1968): "I drank gin-and-hot-water to blunt the pain and took Dexedrine to blunt the gin."

Raymond Chandler had a thing for the gimlet. His preferred preparation for the cocktail is described in *The Long Goodbye* (1953), as detective Philip Marlowe recounts a bar conversation with character Terry Lennox:

> We sat in a corner of the bar at Victor's and drank gimlets. "They don't know how to make them here," he said. "What they call a gimlet is just some lime or lemon juice and gin with a dash of sugar and bitters. A real gimlet is half gin and half Rose's Lime Juice and nothing else. It beats martinis hollow."

THE RAMOS GIN FIZZ

The Ramos gin fizz was a favorite of southern playwright Tennessee Williams, the author of *A Streetcar Named Desire* (1947). The original recipe, created in New Orleans in 1888 by bartender Henry Ramos, calls for shaking the strainer for a full twelve minutes to create a proper foam.

Ramos Gin Fizz

1½ ounces London dry gin

1 medium egg white

¾ ounce simple syrup

½ ounce freshly squeezed lime juice

½ ounce half-and-half

3 dashes orange blossom water
(also called orange flower water)

2 ounces club soda

Orange wedge

Alvin Lustig's 1947 book cover design.

In a cocktail shaker, combine the gin, egg white, simple syrup, lime juice, half-and-half, and orange blossom water. Shake vigorously for at least 1 minute. Strain into a Collins glass with no ice, then add the club soda. The drink will be foamy. Top with any excess foam from the cocktail shaker. Garnish with an orange wedge and serve immediately with a straw.

THE MARTINI LOOMS LARGE

The relative ease of illegal gin production during Prohibition helped popularize the traditional gin martini (and a real martini means gin, not vodka), which would go on to become America's predominant cocktail of the mid-twentieth century.

The martini had no shortage of notable enthusiasts . . .

H. L. Mencken, the American journalist and critic, waxed poetic when calling the martini "the only American invention as perfect as a sonnet."

Probably the most famous utterance in martini lore is attributed, perhaps spuriously, to the Algonquin Round Table stalwart Dorothy Parker:

> I like to have a martini,
> Two at the very most.
> After three I'm under the table,
> After four I'm under my host.

Dorothy Parker.

At Harry's Bar in Venice, Ernest Hemingway drank his own dry variant of the martini using a 15:1 gin-to-vermouth ratio. He dubbed it the Montgomery (after British field marshal Bernard Montgomery, who preferred going into battle with a 15:1 troop advantage).

Ernest Hemingway.

The martini was "the elixir of quietude," according to E. B. White, who once mentioned in a letter to a friend that a single dry martini could effectively dislodge his occasional writer's block.

Patricia Highsmith, author of *The Talented Mr. Ripley* (1955) and no stranger to the martini, began drinking as a student at Barnard College. In an early 1940s diary entry, she wrote about the vital role that booze plays for an artist because it allows one to "see the truth, the simplicity, and the primitive emotions once more."

E. B. White.

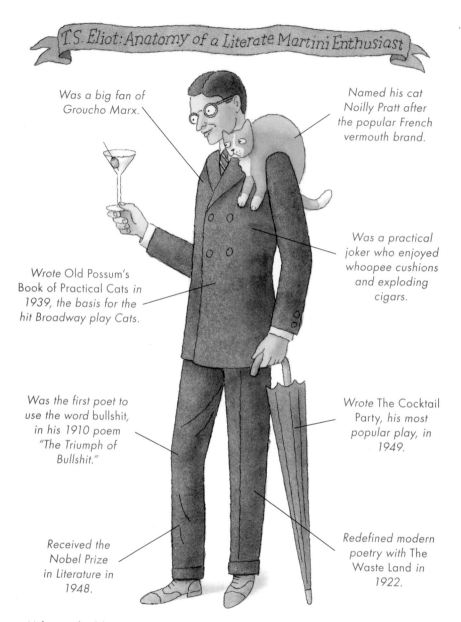

T.S. Eliot: Anatomy of a Literate Martini Enthusiast

Was a big fan of Groucho Marx.

Named his cat Noilly Pratt after the popular French vermouth brand.

Wrote Old Possum's Book of Practical Cats in 1939, the basis for the hit Broadway play Cats.

Was a practical joker who enjoyed whoopee cushions and exploding cigars.

Was the first poet to use the word bullshit, in his 1910 poem "The Triumph of Bullshit."

Wrote The Cocktail Party, his most popular play, in 1949.

Received the Nobel Prize in Literature in 1948.

Redefined modern poetry with The Waste Land in 1922.

When asked by an admirer about the source of his inspiration, T. S. Eliot replied, "Gin and drugs, dear lady, gin and drugs." He would also proclaim, "There is nothing quite so stimulating as a dry martini cocktail."

In *The Letters of T. S. Eliot*, he describes how he wrote the monologue to the verse drama *Sweeney Agonistes*: "I wrote it in three quarters of an hour after church time and before lunch one Sunday morning, with the assistance of half a bottle of Booth's gin."

THE CLASSIC DRY GIN MARTINI

The most iconic glass shape in cocktail history.

As with most legacy cocktails, the martini's origins are disputed. Some drink historians believe that the cocktail's name comes from the Italian vermouth brand Martini & Rossi, which was first marketed in 1863. Others contend that it evolved from a cocktail called the Martinez, which was served at the Occidental Hotel in San Francisco in the early 1860s and named for a nearby town. Another theory traces the martini back to the Knickerbocker Hotel in New York City around 1912.

The "proper" ratio of gin to vermouth in a martini has changed over time as taste preferences have moved to the dryer end of the spectrum (less vermouth). In the 1930s the ratio was 3:1, in the 1940s it was 4:1. By the late twentieth century, it was not uncommon for a bartender to spray just a mist of vermouth into the glass with an atomizer.

Noël Coward, preferring his martinis extremely dry, once declared, "A perfect martini should be made by filling a glass with gin, then waving it in the general direction of Italy (the producer of vermouth)."

Gin Martini

Cracked ice

2½ ounces London dry gin (such as Bombay, Beefeater, or Gordon's)

½ ounce dry vermouth, preferably Noilly Prat

Green olive for garnish

Fill a cocktail shaker or mixing glass with ice. Add the gin and vermouth. Stir well, about 20 seconds, then strain into a martini glass. Garnish with the olive.

BOTANICAL MANIA

Gin, like all traditional spirits, has benefited immensely from the modern craft-cocktail movement. At its core gin is juniper-infused vodka, but after that the botanical variations of gin are endless. Bombay Sapphire kicked things off in 1987, creating the first commercial gin to depart from the classic juniper-forward "London dry" style with a recipe of ten ingredients including almond, lemon peel, orrisroot, and grain of paradise.

Since then innovative microdistillers have run wild, incorporating unusual new botanicals such as white pine, Oregon grape, cumin, lavender, saffron, marionberries, coconut, and seaweed. Faced with sampling the sheer number of disparate gin offerings available today, writers of yesteryear would have been hard-pressed to find time in front of the typewriter.

VODKA

Chapter 5

Vodka goes well with a wintery perspective. Nothing else provokes such presentiments of falling snow, except for some, the communist seizure of the state.

—Michèle Bernstein, *All the King's Horses* (1960)

In Eastern Europe, vodka has been the dominant spirit for centuries. However, its popularity in the West, and particularly the United States, is a relatively recent phenomenon. It didn't gain traction here until the latter half of the twentieth century. Consequently, vodka missed America's Prohibition era, and the beginnings of the great writer/booze confluence of the 1920s. As a result, the literary icons of the Jazz Age were largely unaware of the spirit, and little was drunk or written about it. The Russians, of course, have been writing about vodka for eons. Although late to the party, vodka would eventually get its moment in the sun, ultimately going on to surpass whiskey and gin as the world's top-selling spirit.

THE NATIONAL DRINK OF RUSSIA AND POLAND

As with all spirits, vodka's early history is muddled and the subject of much speculation. With scant historical evidence to support competing claims, just about the only thing that scholars can agree on is that vodka originated either in Poland or in Russia. The spirit plays a seminal role in the drinking history of both countries, but Russia is where it has long been deeply embedded in the national psyche.

BURNT WATER

Potatoes, eventually a key vodka ingredient, didn't arrive in Europe until the sixteenth century.

The name *vodka* is generally acknowledged as a derivative of *voda*, the Slavic word for "little water" (or the Polish *woda*). The first mention of vodka may have appeared in Polish court documents from 1405, but the present usage as a term for a clear ethanol-based spirit didn't achieve wide usage in the Russian language until the middle of the nineteenth century.

Early prototypes of the colorless spirit were distilled from a fermented mash of grain, corn, or grape must, and were produced under a variety of different names including bread wine, distilled wine, *vinum crematum* (Latin for "burnt wine"), and aqua vitae (Latin for "water of life"). Potatoes, eventually a key vodka ingredient, didn't arrive in Europe until the sixteenth century.

POLISH TINCTURE

Poland lays claim to having produced an early prototype of vodka in the eighth century, but this may have been a distillation of wine—more akin to a crude brandy. The first documented evidence of grain-based wines in Russia occurred as early as the ninth century.

Later iterations of Polish vodka appeared in the eleventh century under the name *gorzalka* ("burnt water"—a reference to alcohol produced during the heating process in a still). *Gorzalka* and other vodka antecedents, like most distilled liquors produced then and throughout the Middle Ages, were intended primarily as pharmaceutical tinctures. These early, primitive grain distillates were harsh and cloudy, bearing little resemblance to modern vodka.

Applying bellows to the furnace during distillation, fifteenth century.

One of the earliest mentions of vodka in Polish literature occurs in national poet Adam Mickiewicz's epic poem *Pan Tadeusz* (1834). The poem is a paean to Old Polish culinary traditions. A sample couplet:

The men were given vodka; and all took their seat,
And Lithuanian cold barszcz [borscht] all proceeded to eat.

VODKA'S EARLY MOSCOW YEARS

Ground zero for something akin to modern Russian vodka is hotly debated. According to one theory, the science of distillation was introduced in Moscow in 1386 when ambassadors from Kaffa, a Genoese colony in the Crimea, presented aqua vitae, an aqueous solution of ethanol distilled from grape must, to Grand Prince Dmitry Donskoy.

Grand Prince Dmitry Donskoy.

Another Russian legend maintains that a Russian Orthodox monk named Isidore, from the Chudov Monastery inside the Kremlin in Moscow, concocted the first high-quality recipe for Russian grain vodka around 1430, and dubbed it "bread wine." No historical documentation exists to support this claim.

Grand Prince Ivan III, seeing an enormous revenue opportunity, established state control over vodka production and distribution between 1472 and 1478. This would be the first of many government monopolies on vodka established and repealed over the course of Russian history.

THE BIG EAGLE

In Russia a man's drinking prowess was a measure of his virility. Teetotalers were eyed with suspicion. The eighteenth-century tsar Peter the Great, whose favorite drink was anise-flavored vodka, prided himself on his ability to drink prodigiously without getting drunk and was purportedly impervious to hangovers. As a punishment for guests who arrived late to official court feasts, hoping to avoid excessive drinking, he established what was known as the "penalty shot"—in the form of a 1.5-liter goblet named "the Big Eagle."

In 1863 the state monopoly on vodka was repealed, triggering a drop in prices and making the spirit accessible to all classes. It soon became the drink of choice for most Russians. In the nineteenth century, Russian soldiers fighting in the Napoleonic Wars helped spread vodka across Europe.

THE RUSSIAN SHAKESPEARE

Aleksandr Pushkin, often dubbed "the Russian Shakespeare," was the first of the country's great writers to mention vodka in his work. The spirit's role in Russian life is alluded to in his short story "The Shot" (1830): "The best marksman I ever met used to shoot every day, at least three times before dinner. It was as much a part of his daily routine as a glass of vodka."

It was not uncommon in Russia for children to drink vodka, and not only during social and ceremonial functions. Early introduction to alcohol was believed to prevent alcoholism. In an 1834 letter to his wife regarding their young son, Pushkin wrote: "I'm happy to hear that Sashka has been weaned . . . the fact that the wet nurse was in the habit of drinking before bed is no great misfortune. The boy will grow accustomed to vodka."

DOSTOYEVSKY AND THE LIQUID MENACE

In a marked departure from the West, Russian literature is relatively lacking in the glorification of drink. Many Russian writers have tended to take a dim view of the subject, in light of Russia's long and often woeful history of inebriation.

Fyodor Dostoyevsky.

Alcohol's pernicious effect on the Russian soul was a common theme in the work of Fyodor Dostoyevsky. The original working title for *Crime and Punishment* (1866) was *The Drunkards*. In a letter to his editor, Andrei Krayevsky, Dostoyevsky wrote, "[The novel] will be connected with the current problem of drunkenness. Not only is the problem examined, but all of its ramifications are represented, most of all depictions of families, the bringing up of children under these circumstances, and so on."

In his novel *Demons* (1871), Dostoyevsky declares, "The Russian God has already been vanquished by cheap vodka. The peasants are drunk, the mothers are drunk, the children are drunk, the churches are empty."

Not that Dostoyevsky was above enjoying the spirit himself. Mikhail Alexandrov, a friend and writing colleague, recorded the writer's morning ritual in his diary: "Once when I visited Fyodor Mikhailovich during breakfast, I saw how he consumed simple grain vodka; he bit off some brown bread, took a sip from a glass of vodka, and then chewed it all together."

Russians traditionally enjoy their vodka with food. One of its classic pairings is caviar.

LEO THE KILLJOY

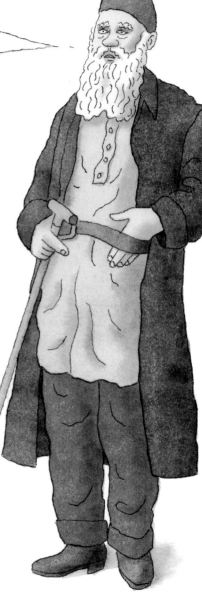

JUST SAY NYET

In a closed society subject to censorship, where vodka, politics, and money have been inextricably bound for centuries, many writers have been reticent to express themselves freely on the subject of drinking. Leo Tolstoy, emboldened by his international celebrity, was not one of them.

The author of *War and Peace* (1869) and *Anna Karenina* (1873) regarded vodka not only as a poison but as a profitable instrument of suppression of the peasantry by the autocracy. In 1887 he founded a temperance society called the Union Against Drunkenness, and in 1890 he penned a famous essay titled "Why Do Men Stupefy Themselves?" In it he wrote: "The cause of the world-wide consumption of hashish, opium, wine, and tobacco, lies not in the taste, nor in any pleasure, recreation, or mirth they afford, but simply in man's need to hide from himself the demands of conscience."

Leo Tolstoy.

THE VODKA AGNOSTIC

Anton Chekov's views on vodka, and alcohol in general, wavered between disdain and sympathy. The great Russian short-fiction writer decried vodka producers as "Satan's blood peddlers"—two of his brothers were alcoholics—but he also understood the human desire for a salve against the harsh realities of daily existence. The heavy drinkers in his stories and plays are rendered with humor and compassion.

After being admonished by his niece for drinking with his doctor, the title character of Chekhov's play *Uncle Vanya* (1896) remarks, "When real life is missing, one must create an illusion."

Anton Chekhov sporting his signature pince-nez.

In Chekov's short story "At Sea: A Sailor's Story" (1883) one of the dissolute protagonists exclaims: "We sailors drink a lot of vodka and sin left and right because we do not know what good virtue does anyone at sea."

THE RUSSIAN BUKOWSKI

And then there was Venedikt Erofeev, the unapologetic vodka enthusiast, known as much for his fondness for the spirit as for his writing. His early Brezhnev-era comic masterpiece, *Moscow to the End of the Line* (1969), depicts one of world literature's most famous alcoholic benders. The pseudo-autobiographical prose poem recounts a vodka-soaked train journey from

Moscow to Petushki taken by a recently fired cable fitter to visit his lover and young son. During the phantasmagoric trip, the narrator, Venichka, engages in philosophical discussions about drinking with fellow travelers, oversleeps and misses his station, and eventually wakes up on a train headed back to Moscow.

Venedikt Erofeev's forward-swept hair predates Justin Bieber.

Alexander Genis, a Russian American author, describes Erofeev as "a great explorer of the metaphysics of drink. For him, alcohol is a concentrated otherworldliness. Intoxication is a means of breaking free, of becoming—literally—not of this world. Vodka is the midwife of the new reality."

Large quantities of Stolichnaya are consumed in Moscow to the End of the Line.

TWENTIETH-CENTURY RUSSIAN
HEADS OF STATE AND VODKA

Vladimir Mayakovsky, the leading poet of the Russian Revolution of 1917, famously said it was "better to die of vodka than of boredom." Russian leaders were not united in their feelings on the subject . . .

In 1914, Tsar Nicholas II, convinced that his inebriated soldiers had cost him the Russo-Japanese War, issued a decree banning the production and sale of alcohol.

Vladimir Lenin declared that "vodka and other narcotics will draw us back to capitalism, rather than forward to Communism," and ordered drunkards to be shot.

Joseph Stalin used vodka sales to finance the socialist industrialization of the Soviet Union.

Nikita Khrushchev's favorite drink was pepper vodka.

Leonid Brezhnev preferred
Zubrówka, a bison-grass-flavored
vodka from Belarus.

Mikhail Gorbachev's first official act
as general secretary in 1985 was
to launch a temperance campaign
restricting access to vodka,
making him hugely unpopular.

His successor, the hard-drinking
Boris Yeltsin, became known for
his vodka-fueled antics on the
world stage.

Today Vladimir Putin is not big on
hard liquor and reportedly prefers
beer to vodka.

VODKA IN AMERICA

Despite the ubiquity of vodka in the United States today—one out of three cocktails ordered in the United States contains the spirit—its early stateside years were rocky. Emerging from Prohibition, Americans already had a favorite colorless spirit—gin. As a relatively flavorless competitor, vodka was a hard sell.

Following the end of Prohibition in 1933, Vladimir Smirnov, the son of the hugely successful Russian distillery founder Pyotr Smirnov, sold the name, recipe, and production rights in the United States to Rudolph Kunett, a Ukranian American. Kunett set up shop in Bethel, Connecticut, but was unprepared for America's indifference to the liquor. After five fruitless years, he sold the business to John G. Martin, the president of Heublein Inc. for fourteen thousand dollars.

John G. Martin, the man who made vodka popular in the United States.

One of Martin's marketing gimmicks was to serve the Moscow mule in a copper mug.

Sales remained flat for several years, but in 1941, Martin traveled to Los Angeles and met Jack Morgan, owner of the Hollywood restaurant the Cock'n Bull. Morgan had a surplus of British ginger beer he'd been unable to sell. With two products on their hands that nobody wanted, they tried mixing vodka with ginger beer, and the result was the Moscow mule. The cocktail's instant success was the American foothold the spirit needed. Bartenders suddenly saw its enormous potential as a neutral mixing agent.

THE VODKA TONIC

Unlike their Eastern European counterparts who drink vodka neat, most Western devotees have preferred the spirit diluted with another beverage, or as the active ingredient in a cocktail.

American writer and Beat Generation icon William S. Burroughs, who once said, "Our national drug is alcohol," was often spotted in later years consuming his signature vodka and Coke.

The most enduring vodka mixer has been tonic water. Christopher Isherwood, the English American novelist, worried about drinking too many of them. The author, whose *Berlin Stories* (1945) is set in the boozy, libertine years leading up to the rise of Hitler, was acutely mindful of the potential long-term damage to his health. In his posthumously published diaries (1996) he often begins his entries with "Today I'm going to stop smoking and drinking vodka tonics."

Christopher Isherwood.

Another fan of the vodka tonic was Pete Hamill, the hard-drinking NYC journalist who was a regular at the Greenwich Village tavern the Lion's Head. At the legendary literary bar Hamill traded stories with the likes of Frank McCourt, Seamus Heaney, and Norman Mailer. In his memoir *A Drinking Life* (1995), Hamill writes: "I don't think many New York bars ever had such a glorious mixture of newspapermen, painters, musicians, seamen, ex-communists, priests and nuns, athletes, stockbrokers, politicians, and folksingers, bound together in the leveling democracy of drink." But at thirty-eight, Hamill acknowledged the toll on his body and mind and hung up his shot glass for good. His last drink in 1972 was a vodka tonic.

Several blocks away from the Lion's Head (shuttered in 1996) in Greenwich Village was the legendary White Horse Tavern, a literary stomping ground in the 1950s and '60s for such notables as Jack Kerouac, Anaïs Nin, James Baldwin, Norman Mailer, and Hunter S. Thompson.

SHAKEN NOT STIRRED

Novelist Ian Fleming would inadvertently boost vodka sales in the 1960s when his fictional British Secret Service agent James Bond transitioned to the silver screen. In the films Bond's signature drink was the vodka martini, shaken not stirred. Prior to Bond, ordering a martini meant a gin martini. Shaking, so the theory went, would "bruise" the gin—but apparently vodka wasn't so delicate.

However, the Bond of Fleming's books wasn't quite so adamant about vodka—he often ordered gin martinis as well. In the first title of the series, *Casino Royale* (1953), Bond orders a vesper, containing both vodka and gin, with precise instructions to the bartender: "Three measures of Gordon's [gin], one of vodka, half a measure of Kina Lillet. Shake it very well until it's ice-cold, then add a large thin slice of lemon peel. Got it?"

Ian Fleming's James Bond.

Contemporary novelist and fellow Brit Lawrence Osborne also enjoys a well-made vodka martini. In the *The Wet and the Dry* (2013) he revels in the danger associated with drinking in the largely dry countries of the Middle East. Sitting in Le Bristol Hotel in Beirut, with an armed soldier stationed outside the revolving glass doors, he describes the inconspicuous bar as "an exercise in discretion," before slipping into his vodka martini: "Salty like cold seawater at the bottom of an oyster, the drink strikes you as sinister and cool and satisfying to the nerves, because it takes a certain nerve to drink it."

SCREWDRIVER

The screwdriver—orange juice and vodka—was Truman Capote's tipple of choice. The author of *Breakfast at Tiffany's* (1958) and *In Cold Blood* (1966) referred to it as "my orange drink."

According to Victorino Matus, author of *Vodka: How a Colorless, Odorless, Flavorless Spirit Conquered America* (2014), the cocktail got its name from American oil rig workers in the Persian Gulf in the late 1940s. While on the job, they discreetly added vodka to their orange juice and stirred with the closest implement on hand—a screwdriver.

Screwdriver

Ice
2 ounces vodka
Orange juice
Orange wedge for garnish

In a highball glass with ice, pour in the vodka and fill with orange juice. Garnish with the orange wedge.

WHERE I'M DRINKING FROM

Raymond Carver was called the "the Chekhov of Middle America" by the *Times of London*. Carver, whose spare prose did much to reinvigorate the American short story in the 1980s, was also, for most of his adult life, hopelessly in the thrall of vodka. But unlike so many of his alcoholic forebears, he was eventually able to walk away from it.

Carver grew up in the small town of Yakima, in eastern Washington, where his father worked in a sawmill. Both of his parents drank, and he got his first taste of alcohol as a child. In a 1983 interview with the *Paris Review*, he recounted the experience:

> "In the cabinet under the kitchen sink, [my mother] kept a bottle of patent 'nerve medicine,' and she'd take a couple of tablespoons of this every morning. My dad's nerve medicine was whiskey. . . . I remember sneaking a taste of it once and hating it, and wondering how anybody could drink the stuff."

Carver started smoking in his early teens to help combat a weight problem. His parents often bought him his own carton so he wouldn't mooch from theirs.

His first published story was called "Pastoral," which appeared in the *Western Humanities Review* in 1963. He was thrilled that Charles Bukowski had a poem in the same issue.

While teaching in Iowa in 1973 with fellow Chekhovian inebriate John Cheever, Carver later wrote that "he and I did nothing *but* drink. . . . We met our classes in a manner of speaking, but the entire time we were there . . . I don't think either of us ever took the covers off our typewriters."

John Cheever, "the Chekhov of the Suburbs."

THE STORIES OF RAYMOND CARVER WILL YOU PLEASE BE QUIET, PLEASE?

According to his biographer, Carol Sklenicka, Carver drank vodka at his dining room table while correcting the printer's galleys for his first book of short stories, *Will You Please Be Quiet, Please?* (1976).

First edition, 1976, published by McGraw-Hill, New York.

Carver's drinking wrecked his first marriage, to Maryann Burk Carver. In her 2006 memoir, *What It Used to Be Like: A Portrait of My Marriage to Raymond Carver*, Maryann recounts a drunken episode where he cracked her over the head with his vodka bottle, nearly killing her.

In 1977, after two visits to a recovery center and three to a hospital, Carver gave up drinking. His friend Douglas Unger, the American novelist, has said, "Ray confessed several times that he wasn't sure if, in sobriety, he would ever be able to write again."

In fact, his final eleven years sober turned out to be his most productive, culminating in the publication of his landmark collection *Cathedral* (1984). Included in the collection was the award-winning story "Where I'm Calling From," which focuses on an alcoholic at a "drying-out facility." J.P., the narrator, invokes Jack London's story "To Build a Fire" as a metaphor for recovery—he can either freeze to death or choose life by building a fire.

First edition, 1983, published by Alfred E. Knopf, New York.

Reflecting back on his drinking in the *Paris Review* interview, Carver said: "Of course there's a mythology that goes along with the drinking, but I was never into that. I was into the drinking itself. I suppose I began to drink heavily after I'd realized that the things I wanted most in life for myself and my writing, and my wife and my children, were simply not going to happen."

In his essay "Raymond Carver and the Ethos of Drinking," David McCracken remarks that in many of Carver's stories his characters paradoxically rely on alcohol to treat the very problems caused by their alcohol dependence. He writes: "In Carver's fictional universe, drinking gives many characters a sense of stability through which they can evaluate their lives, even if this stability is fleeting."

Carver, also a heavy cigarette smoker, died in 1988 of lung cancer.

Carver referred to the version of himself during his drinking days as "Bad Raymond."

THE BLOODY MARY

Industrious writers who drink heavily inevitably must contend with the biggest obstacle to resuming work the next day: the hangover. Ernest Hemingway and Raymond Carver preferred the "hair of the dog" approach, usually in the form of a bloody mary.

The popular creation story for the drink is that, in the 1920s, bartender Fernand "Pete" Petiot first mixed vodka and tomato juice at Harry's New York Bar in Paris.

In 1934, after Prohibition, Petiot helmed the King Cole Bar at New York's St. Regis Hotel, where he introduced a similar drink consisting of vodka, tomato juice, citrus, and spices. The hotel's owner, Vincent Astor, objected to the name bloody mary, so the drink was initially dubbed the red snapper.

A comedian named George Jessel also claimed to have created the drink, at the Palm Beach restaurant La Maze in 1927. The name purportedly arose when a socialite spilled the drink down the front of her white gown, exclaiming, "Now you can call me Bloody Mary, George!"

Another popular, and uncorroborated, theory holds that the cocktail's moniker was borrowed from the murderous sixteenth-century persecutor of Protestants, Queen Mary Tudor.

Yet another debunked myth attributes the drink's genesis to Hemingway. He may not have created it, but he did concoct his own recipe, as recorded in *Ernest Hemingway: Selected Letters, 1917–1961* (1981). His version calls for a pitcher because "any smaller amount is worthless":

Ernest Hemingway's Bloody Mary

Ice
16 ounces good Russian vodka
16 ounces chilled tomato juice
1 tablespoon Worcester sauce (Lea and Perrins)
1½ ounce freshly squeezed lime juice
Celery salt
Cayenne pepper
Black pepper

In a pitcher half filled with ice, mix the vodka and tomato juice. Add the Worcester sauce and stir. Add the lime juice and stir. Add small amounts of celery salt, cayenne pepper, and black pepper. Stir and taste. If too powerful, weaken with more tomato juice. If it lacks authority, add more vodka.

He adds at the end: "For combatting a really terrific hangover increase the amount of Worcester sauce—but don't lose the lovely color."

SWEDEN AND ABSOLUT VODKA

Lars Olsson Smith.

Although Sweden did not adopt the designation of "vodka" until the 1950s, it too had been producing the spirit for centuries under the name *brännvin* ("burn-wine"). The country's most famous brand, Absolut, was founded in 1879 by Lars Olsson Smith.

In 1979, under the guidance of entrepreneur Peter Ekelund and master distiller Börje Karlsson, Absolut was rebranded for a global launch that would alter the face of the spirits industry. Due in large part to the company's ingenious advertising campaign, vodka in general would eventually eclipse scotch, gin, and wine in units sold worldwide.

YEARNING FOR THE GOOD OLD DAYS

Gary Shteyngart.

Like Misha Vainberg, the protagonist in his best-selling novel *Absurdistan* (2006), Gary Shteyngart likes his vodka. Shteyngart was raised in Leningrad before immigrating to New York City at age seven, and true to his Russian roots, he prefers to drink vodka neat. His favorite brand is Russian Standard. "It doesn't have a story about how it's been triple-filtered through a diamond in a rhinoceros's asshole, but it gets the job done."

In a 2006 interview with *Modern Drunkard Magazine*, Shteyngart laments the demise of the literary drinking tradition:

> It's so hard to be a writer these days. It's so antiseptic. We're this sterilized profession, we all know our Amazon.com rankings to the nearest digit. . . .
> . . . There are so few people to drink with. The literary community is not backing me up here. I'm all alone. . . .
> . . . The world I live in, in my mind, is still the world of F. Scott Fitzgerald and Hemingway. And Dostoyevsky. Drink it all away or gamble it all away at the drop of a hat. That doesn't exist anymore."

THE TASTELESS TITAN

Lawrence Osborne observes that vodka has become "the most successful man-made drug of all time." Yet, despite its current supremacy as the world's largest internationally traded spirit, drink purists (and writers outside of the Russian sphere of influence) have never really warmed up to it.

Vodka connoisseurs notwithstanding, the drink's popularity lies not in what it possesses but in what it lacks—flavor. Proudly wearing its tastelessness on its sleeve, vodka has never inspired the hushed reverence associated with other fine spirits. Kingsley Amis, in Every Day Drinking, bemoans the underwhelming impression vodka leaves on the palate, explaining that it's "for the benefit of those second-rate persons who don't like the taste of gin, or indeed that of drink in general."

ABSINTHE

Chapter 6

Absinthe has a lovely colour, green. A glass of absinthe is as poetic as every other thing. What difference is there between a glass of absinthe and a sunset?

—Oscar Wilde (as told by Christian Krohg in *In Little Day Trips to and from Paris*, 1897)

Describing absinthe in his 1913 compendium of satirical definitions, Dictionnaire des idées reçues, Gustave Flaubert writes: "Extra-violent poison: a glass and you're dead. Journalists drink it while they write their articles. Killed more soldiers than the Bedouins."

Absinthe may be the most vilified, and misunderstood, spirit in the history of drink. No beverage has engendered more public hysteria, collective hand-wringing, or spurious claims. As such, the liquor also bears the distinction of being the most widely banned spirit of the last two hundred years.

And not surprisingly, thanks to its dangerous reputation, no other drink has been more romanticized or mythologized—or closely linked to the creative spirit. Numerous writers, poets, painters, and composers have all fallen under the sway of "the Green Muse."

Poet Paul Verlaine dubbed the drink "the Green Fairy."

118

WORMWOOD

The key ingredient in absinthe is *Artemisia absinthium*, better known as wormwood, a woody perennial plant native to Mediterranean regions of Eurasia and northern Africa. Its distinctive green color comes from chlorophyll in the macerated wormwood leaves used to create the drink.

Wormwood-infused spirits can be traced back to ancient Egypt, Greece, and Rome, where they were used primarily for medicinal purposes. In *Naturalis historia* (circa AD 77), Pliny the Elder detailed the many ailments wormwood could treat, as well as the many ways to prepare it, including a wormwood wine made by soaking the stems and leaves with grape must.

Wormwood.

The word *vermouth* is derived from the German *Wermut* (wormwood). Vermouth, in its earliest form, was a wormwood-infused fortified wine produced in Germany and Hungary in the sixteenth century. Wormwood can still be found in some modern vermouth recipes.

The Swiss canton of Neuchâtel.

But the prototype for modern absinthe would come centuries later, originating in the Swiss canton of Neuchâtel during the latter half of the eighteenth century. When French symbolist poet Arthur Rimbaud called absinthe the "sagebrush of the glaciers," he was referring to Val-de-Travers, a chilly district within the canton where wormwood was plentiful.

THE MYSTERIOUS ELIXIR OF VAL-DE-TRAVERS

Although the birthplace of absinthe is not in dispute, the individuals responsible for its creation are shrouded in myth and mystery. Scholars today are still trying to separate the messy tangle of facts from the fiction.

The most widely circulated legend involves a French military deserter named Pierre Ordinaire, who fled to the Swiss village of Couvet in Val-de-Travers in 1767. There he donned the guise of a country doctor (his medical credentials were dubious), gaining a favorable reputation after dispensing an herbal remedy composed of wormwood and aromatic plants. Many of his patients declared themselves radically cured after drinking the mysterious elixir. Another version of this story suggests that Ordinaire didn't concoct the drink himself but co-opted the recipe from a local herbalist named Mademoiselle Henriod, who had already been selling the wormwood elixir for some time. The existence of an absinthe bottle from the time, labeled with the inscription "Superior quality absinthe extract from the single recipe of Marguerite Henriette Henriod," supports the theory.

Marguerite Henriette Henriod.

Henri-Louis Pernod.

In 1798 a French merchant and customer of Henriod's, Major Daniel Henri Dubied-Duval, recognizing the commercial potential of her elixir, established *Dubied Père et Fils,* the first mass-production absinthe distillery in Couvet, with the youngest of his five sons, Marcelin, and his son-in-law Henri-Louis Pernod.

In 1802, in order to optimize the distribution of their product, Henri and Marcelin established Pernod Fils & Dubied in Pontarlier, France, near the Swiss border. After a split in their partnership in 1804, Henri joined forces with David Auguste Boiteux to established Pernod Fils & Boiteux Distillery. This would become one of the most popular brands of absinthe up until 1914, when the drink was banned in France.

FRENCH MEDICINE

Absinthe was marketed as a health tonic by Pernod and other producers, and the French military adopted it for medicinal purposes. During the French conquest of Algeria (1830–1847), soldiers were provided regular field rations of absinthe to ward off fevers, malaria, and dysentery. Of course, they were soon drinking it for nonmedicinal purposes as well. Soldiers who survived the war took their thirst for the powerful intoxicant back home with them, sparking an upsurge in production all over France.

THE GREAT FRENCH WINE BLIGHT

The Phylloxera *aphid as depicted in an Edward Sambourne cartoon from* Punch, *1890.*

In the mid-nineteenth century a massive outbreak of phylloxera (a vine-eating aphid) swept French vineyards, causing the *Great French Wine Blight,* which nearly wiped out the country's wine industry, causing the prices to skyrocket. The 1863 infestation was not effectively halted until the 1890s. The resulting wine shortage turned out to be a boon for the absinthe industry. Before the blight, the spirit had been a pricey indulgence reserved for the middle classes, but absinthe producers quickly stepped in to fill the wine void. Along with a massive increase in production came a sharp drop in price. The Green Fairy was suddenly accessible to a burgeoning bohemian subculture of writers, poets, and artists who could no longer afford wine.

THE GREEN HOUR

Absinthe helped fuel the spread of café culture throughout Europe—by 1869, thousands of cabarets and cafés existed in Paris alone. The drink became fashionable as a potent aperitif consumed in mid-to-late afternoon, and this time of day soon became known as *l'heure verte* ("the green hour"). Another byproduct of absinthe's growing popularity was the street prostitution that organized around cafés and the green hour. The café, previously an institution known for political and intellectual exchange, was now becoming a center for pleasure as well.

A ritual developed around the consumption of absinthe (giving rise to a fetishistic appetite for absinthe-related paraphernalia):

1. The liqueur was poured into a special glass fashioned with a bulb or bubble for measuring the precise ratio of absinthe to cold water.

2. A flat, often beautifully designed, perforated spoon was placed across the rim of the glass.

3. A sugar cube was placed on the spoon.

4. Cold water was slowly poured over the sugar cube.

Part of the drink's appeal was aesthetic—as water was added to the absinthe, the deep green color of the liquor turned milky and iridescent.

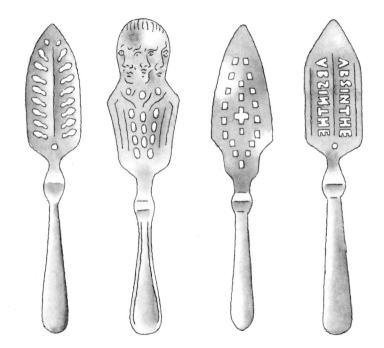

Mixologists have created numerous cocktail recipes featuring absinthe, but the basic water-drip preparation is the classic way to drink it.

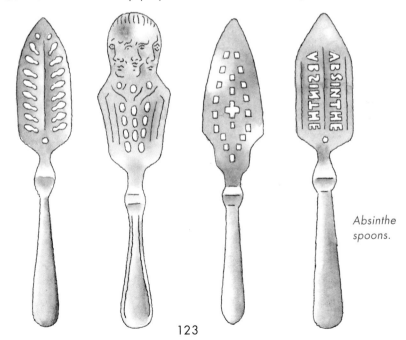

Absinthe spoons.

BOHEMIAN RHAPSODY

Absinthe reached its zenith of popularity during the Belle Époque (typically dated from the end of the Franco-Prussian War in 1871 to the outbreak of World War I in 1914) in Paris, where a constellation of distinguished writers, artists, and musicians succumbed to the allure of the Green Fairy. They were part of a revolutionary counterculture movement that rejected classical idealization in the arts in favor of a gritty realism that crossed class and gender lines.

A cancan dancer from the legendary Parisian cabaret Moulin Rouge, founded in 1889.

The French poet and novelist Henri Murger's *Scènes de la vie de bohème* (1845), as well as French composer George Bizet's opera *Carmen* (1876), did much to popularize the so-called bohemian lifestyle of the counterculture movement. The decadence and heavy drinking of many of the artists involved would eventually sully absinthe's reputation, but it did little to tarnish our cultural fascination with the bohemian demimonde.

Absinthe still manufactured in Paris, 1881.

LA VIE BOHÈME:
THE WRITERS AND ARTISTS OF MONTMARTRE

The Montmartre district of Paris, situated on a large hill in the city's Eighteenth Arrondissement, was Europe's bohemian epicenter. Absinthe flowed freely at *Le Chat Noir* in Montmartre, founded in 1881 by impresario Rodolphe Salis and considered the first modern cabaret. Paul Verlaine, Spanish painter Pablo Picasso, and French composer Erik Satie were among Le Chat Noir's many illustrious patrons.

The iconic 1896 poster by Théophile Steinlen promoting Le Chat Noir's troupe of cabaret entertainers.

Henri de Toulouse-Lautrec.

Henri de Toulouse-Lautrec was another regular, and he was known for keeping glass vials of absinthe in the hollowed-out custom-made canes that he carried, referred to today as "Toulouse-Lautrec" or "tippling" canes. One of his favorite cocktails was called the earthquake, a mixture of absinthe and Cognac.

The "tippling" cane.

125

In Charles Baudelaire's "The Poison," from his 1857 collection of poetry *Les fleurs du mal* (*The Flowers of Evil*), absinthe (the poison of the title) ranks above wine and opium:

> All that is not equal to the poison which flows
> From your eyes, from your green eyes,
> Lakes where my soul trembles and sees its evil side . . .
> My dreams come in multitude
> To slake their thirst in those bitter gulfs.

French symbolist writer Alfred Jarry, best known for his play *Ubu roi* (*King Ubu*) (1896), insisted on drinking his absinthe straight, referring to it as "holy water."

Alfred Jarry.

Guy de Maupassant partook, as did many of his characters in short stories such as "A Queer Night in Paris": "M. Saval sat down at some distance from them and waited, for the hour of taking absinthe was at hand."

Fellow symbolist and Dutch poet Gustave Kahn (1859–1936) expressed his devotion in free verse:

Absinthe, mother of all happiness,
O infinite liquor, you glint in my glass green
and pale like the eyes of the mistress
I once loved. . . .

The hirsute Gustave Kahn.

Edgar Degas's famous 1876 painting *L'absinthe*, which hangs in the Musée d'Orsay in Paris, portrays two of his friends drinking at their favorite haunt, the *Café de la Nouvelles Athènes* on the Place Pigalle.

In writing his novel *L'assommoir*, a study of alcoholism among the poor of Paris, the French writer Émile Zola credited Degas for some the book's imagery, telling him, "I quite plainly described some of your pictures in more than one place in my pages."

Émile Zola.

Nana, the prostitute from Zola's novel by the same name (1880), drinks absinthe to forget "the beastliness of men."

French poet Raoul Ponchon declares in his 1886 poem "Absinthe":

Absinthe, I adore you, truly!
It seems, when I drink you,
I inhale the young forest's soul,
During the beautiful green season.

Your perfume disconcerts me
And in your opalescence
I see the full heavens of yore
As through an open door.

Raoul Ponchon.

French painter Paul Gaugin, in a letter to a friend in 1897, wrote: "I sit at my door, smoking a cigarette and sipping my absinthe, and I enjoy every day without a care in the world."

Vincent Van Gogh was introduced to the spirit by Toulouse-Lautrec and Gaugin. Historians speculate that he may have been addicted to chemicals of the turpene class—present in camphor, turpentine, and absinthe. This craving would explain his known propensity to ingest paint and turpentine as well as absinthe.

Picasso arrived in Paris in 1901 at age twenty and went on to create numerous paintings depicting absinthe drinkers, including *Woman Drinking Absinthe* (1901), from his so-called blue period.

One of six copies of Glass of Absinthe, sculptures cast in bronze, each decorated uniquely, by Pablo Picasso, Paris 1914.

PARISIAN PARTY ANIMALS

Absinthe mythology owes much to the tempestuous relationship between poets Arthur Rimbaud and Paul Verlaine, who cut a drunken swath through bohemian Paris. Rimbaud, the enfant terrible, would come to embody the danger, mystery, and romance associated with the liquor. Allen Ginsberg later called Rimbaud "the first punk," and an inspiration for the Beat movement of the 1950s. Rimbaud would also influence the surrealists, and later songwriters such as Bob Dylan, Jim Morrison, and Patti Smith. Verlaine's fame, although he enjoyed an esteemed literary reputation in his day, will forever be linked to Rimbaud.

Arthur Rimbaud.

In 1871, at age seventeen, a then unknown Arthur Rimbaud, from the Ardennes region of France, sent some of his poems to several established poets in Paris. Among the poems included in his correspondence was the now famous "Le bateau ivre" ("The Drunken Boat"), written when he was sixteen.

Paul Verlaine.

His only response came from Paul Verlaine, a distinguished symbolist poet who was fourteen years his senior. He was intrigued by the precocious young talent, and invited Rimbaud to Paris. "Come dear great soul. We await you; we desire you," he wrote back, then sent him a one-way ticket.

Although few references to absinthe appear in Rimbaud's work, it is well known that he became entranced by the Green Fairy soon after meeting Verlaine. The duo became regulars at Le Café du Rat Mort (the Dead Rat Café) on the Place Pigalle in Paris, gaining a reputation around the city for their drunken antics and boorish behavior. Verlaine once said, "If I drink, it is to get drunk, not to drink."

Rimbaud considered the consumption of alcohol and other intoxicants, such as hashish, not as a recreational pursuit but as essential to his writing process. He was looking for a new poetic language. Before departing for Paris he had written to a friend: "The poet makes himself a seer by a long, prodigious, and rational disordering of the senses." In Paris, absinthe was a readily available means to this end.

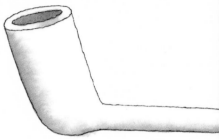

The ubiquitous clay pipe seen in visual depictions of Rimbaud was a Scouflaire, a popular French brand of the time.

The London flat at 8 Royal College Street, where the two poets lived briefly in 1873.

Despite Verlaine's marriage to Mathilde Mauté, he and Rimbaud engaged in a brief but turbulent love affair. Verlaine was enchanted by the younger poet's restless genius and libertine excesses. Rimbaud, in a role reversal, saw himself as Verlaine's mentor, urging the older poet to purge his work of its sentimental bourgeois sensibilities.

Verlaine abandoned his wife and infant child in 1872 to roam around northern France and Belgium with Rimbaud. The two quarreled often, and in 1873 Rimbaud needed a break, decamping to his family's farm in Roche. There he wrote a large portion of his extended prose poem *Une saison en enfer (A Season in Hell)*.

Les poivrots (Drunkards). Verlaine is depicted (by the artist Gustave-Henri Jossot) on a 1907 cover of L'Assiette au Beurre, a French satirical magazine.

Several weeks later he rejoined Verlaine, and they traveled together through London and Belgium. Their stormy relationship ended violently in Brussels when Verlaine, in a drunken jealous rage, fired two shots from a revolver, wounding Rimbaud in the left wrist. Verlaine was arrested and served two years in prison, where he renounced his bohemian life and converted to Catholicism.

The most famous gun in French literature—the Lefaucheux revolver that Verlaine used to shoot Rimbaud—was sold at Christie's auction house in 2016 for $460,000.

For the next two years Rimbaud worked on his groundbreaking suite of prose poems, *Illuminations*, before abandoning poetry altogether at age twenty-one. He then disappeared, wandering around the Horn of Africa on foot and supporting himself as a trader and an arms dealer. He succumbed to bone cancer in Marseilles at age thirty-seven.

Rimbaud's complete works were published in 1895 under Verlaine's supervision, making the deceased poet famous. Absinthe remained Verlaine's truest companion until the end of his days. He died an alcoholic, and in poverty, in Paris at the age of fifty-one.

ABSINTHE IN AMERICA

Absinthe found its way to America in 1837, by way of "the Little Paris of North America," New Orleans. It was first served at a saloon called Aleix's Coffee House, which became known around town as the Absinthe Room. Later, in 1890, it was officially rechristened the Old Absinthe House. The bar eventually became a local landmark, where

The sazerac.

the sazerac, a Cognac/absinthe concoction regarded by some drink historians as America's oldest cocktail, was served to the likes of Mark Twain, William Thackeray, Walt Whitman, and Oscar Wilde.

THE PICTURE OF DORIAN GREEN

Oscar Wilde occupies a central position in absinthe lore due to several memorable descriptions of the drink that are attributed to him. However, none of these quotes can be traced to anything he wrote but rather to hearsay from friends and other writers.

Oscar Wilde.

Wilde fled to France in 1897 following his release from prison in England on indecency charges. The famed author of *The Picture of Dorian Gray* (1890) and *The Importance of Being Earnest* (1895) was not known to be a heavy drinker, and was likely introduced to absinthe in his adopted country.

One of Wilde's most famous musings on the subject is recounted by his friend Ada Leverson, in her book *Letters to the Sphinx from Oscar Wilde: With Reminiscences of the Author* (1930). It concerns how absinthe alters the imbiber's perception of the world: "After the first glass you see things as you wish they were. After the second, you see things as they are not. Finally you see things as they really are, and that is the most horrible thing in the world."

HUH?

Among the many myths that continue to circulate around Edgar Allan Poe is that he was a heavy absinthe drinker. Absinthe consumption may dovetail with the unhinged-artist narrative, but no evidence exists to suggest he drank it, or was even aware of it.

DEVIL IN A BOTTLE

By the late 1800s, absinthe's rise in popularity was accompanied by increasing hysteria and opposition to the drink as a societal menace. Much like the PCP epidemic of the 1970s, or the *Reefer Madness* panic of the 1930s, all manner of wild and erratic behavior was ascribed to its alleged psychoactive properties. The spirit, containing a chemical toxin called thujone (the active ingredient in wormwood oil), was believed to disrupt the central nervous system.

An 1869 pharmaceutical journal in London quoted from a *Pall Mall Gazette* article detailing the ill effects of absinthe drinking:

> After a while the digestive organs become deranged. . . . Now ensues a constant feeling of uneasiness, a painful anxiety, accompanied by sensations of giddiness and tinglings in the ears; and as the day declines, hallucinations of sight and hearing begin. . . . his brain affected by a sort of sluggishness which indicates approaching idiocy . . . in the end come entire loss of intellect, general paralysis, and death.

It has often been suggested that the ingestion of thujone, by way of absinthe consumption, may have exacerbated Vincent Van Gogh's psychosis, thus precipitating the infamous ear-slicing episode of 1888. The truth may never be known, however, the incident was later used as propaganda in the anti-absinthe campaign.

Vincent Van Gogh.

English novelist Maria Corelli's *Wormwood: A Drama of Paris* (1890) follows a promising young Parisian man who falls prey to absinthe's seductive, and ultimately ruinous, powers. The novel's lurid tale of debauchery, murder, suicide, and addiction pandered to British Francophobia, as well as the public's fascination with fin-de-siècle Parisian decadence.

"Absinthe is death!," a poster by F. Monod, 1905.

In 1905 a Swiss farmer named Jean Lanfray shot his wife after a day of drinking wine, Cognac, and absinthe. The press sensationalized the crime, dubbing it "the absinthe murder." Europe's temperance movement seized upon the incident and demonized the spirit as not only a health peril but a moral contaminant. The panic that ensued led to petitions calling to ban the liquor. Belgium outlawed absinthe in 1905, followed by Switzerland and the Netherlands in 1910 and the United States in 1912. France tried raising taxes on absinthe in hopes of depressing demand (in 1907 the spirit contributed sixty million francs in taxes to French coffers), before finally succumbing to a ban in 1915.

After being forced to comply with anti-wormwood laws, absinthe producer Pernod created his famous pastis in 1922, still popular today. It retains the anise character of absinthe but without the wormwood.

The Slain Green Fairy, from a 1910 satirical poster by artist Albert Gantner, critical of the ban on absinthe in prohibitionist Switzerland—the blue cross was the symbol of La Croix Bleue, a powerful temperance organization.

HEMINGWAY AND ABSINTHE

First edition, Charles Scribner's Sons, New York, 1940.

Absinthe could still be obtained illicitly in Paris following the ban, but Ernest Hemingway most likely made his acquaintance with the spirit while working on assignment in Spain, one of the few European countries where it remained legal.

The Green Fairy makes an appearance in *The Sun Also Rises*—the smitten Jake Barnes drinks absinthe to numb the pain following Lady Brett's tryst with a Spanish bullfighter.

Hemingway would enjoy absinthe while working as a journalist covering the Spanish Civil War in the late 1930s. And the spirit again finds its way into his novel inspired by the experience, *For Whom the Bell Tolls* (1940)—his character Robert Jordan sips absinthe from his canteen as a respite from war: "One cup of it took the place of the evening papers, of all the old evenings in cafés, of all chestnut trees that would be in bloom now in this month . . . of all the things he had enjoyed and forgotten and that came back to him when he tasted that opaque, bitter, tongue-numbing, brain-warming, stomach-warming, idea-changing liquid alchemy."

A 1935 book entitled *So Red the Nose: or—Breath in the Afternoon,* a compilation of cocktail recipes by famous authors, included a recipe from Hemingway called "Death in the Afternoon." The drink took its name from Hemingway's 1932 book of the same name about Spanish bullfighting: "Pour one jigger absinthe into a Champagne glass. Add iced Champagne until it attains the proper opalescent milkiness. Drink three to five of these slowly."

An editor's note at the end of the recipe states, "After six of these cocktails *The Sun Also Rises.*"

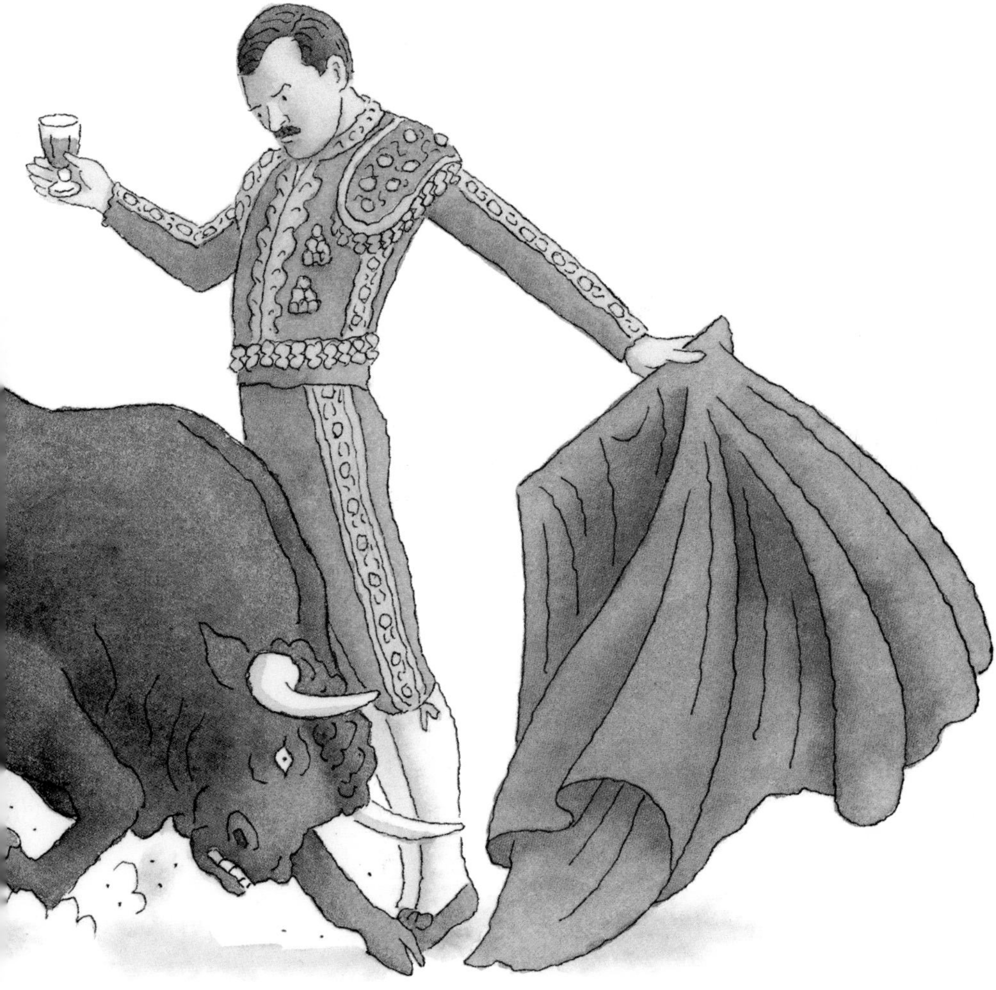

THE GREEN FAIRY REVIVAL

Changing attitudes have led to the relaxation and overturning of laws banning absinthe. In 1988 the European Union made the spirit legal again, so long as thujone content did not exceed ten milligrams/ kilograms. The modern absinthe revival was sparked in the 1990s when British importer BBH Spirits, recognizing that the United Kingdom had never formally banned the spirit, began importing Hill's Absinth from the Czech Republic. This "Bohemian-style absinthe" had little resemblance to classic absinthe but paved the way for brands more faithful to original recipes.

In 2005, Switzerland, absinthe's country of origin, made it legal again to manufacture and sell the spirit (after years of bootlegged production). In 2007, under pressure from distillers and distributers, the United States became the last major Western country to lift the ban. In late 2007 the first American absinthe brand, St. George Absinthe Verte from the St. George distillery in California, made its debut, opening the door for the numerous microdistilleries around the country that now produce it.

Absinthe's heyday as an enigmatic bohemian muse is long over, but today it enjoys a modest resurgence as both fabled icon and hipster curiosity.

MEZCAL & TEQUILA

Chapter 7

Tequila, scorpion honey, harsh dew of the doglands, essence of Aztec, crema de cacti; tequila, oily and thermal like the sun in solution; tequila, liquid geometry of passion; Tequila, the buzzard god who copulates in midair with the ascending souls of dying virgins; tequila, firebug in the house of good taste; O tequila, savage water of sorcery, what confusion and mischief your sly, rebellious drops do generate!

> —Tom Robbins,
> *Still Life with Woodpecker* (1980)

In spite of a rich history that goes back centuries to pre-Columbian times, mezcal (or mescal)—and its best-known style, tequila—remained largely unknown outside of Mexico prior to World War I.

Late Aztec period (AD 1350–1520) ceramic pulque vessel.

Consequently, its backstory as a creative lubricant for modern-era writers in North America and Europe doesn't run nearly as deep or as wide as the other spirits written about in this volume. Today mezcal and tequila are treasured symbols of Mexico's national identity.

Mayahuel is the Aztec goddess of the maguey plant and fertility and was often depicted with many breasts—a reference to the milky sap of the plant.

THE MESOAMERICAN NECTAR OF THE GODS

The story of mezcal begins around 1000 BC with the Aztecs, Mayans, Huastecs, and other cultures in ancient Mesoamerica fermenting the sap of the agave plant, also known as maguey, to create a milky drink called pulque. According to ancient myth, the sacred beverage was bestowed upon humankind by the Aztec deity Quetzalcoatl to lift spirits. Pulque was the forerunner of modern mezcal and tequila.

Quezalcoatl as depicted in the sixteenth-century Codex Maglabechiano, an Aztec religious document.

For more than two thousand years the indigenous people of the Aztec Empire enjoyed the drink all to themselves, until Hernán Cortés and company arrived in 1521 to spoil the party. In between raping and plundering, the Spanish conquistadors found time to enjoy the local beverage.

They liked it enough to attempt shipping it back to Spain, however, due to agave's bacterial composition, the pulque soured too quickly to survive the long voyage across the Atlantic.

Hernán Cortés.

MEXICO'S EARLY DISTILLERIES

In the 1600s the marquis of Altamira built the first large-scale tequila distillery in what is now Tequila, Jalisco. The region's climate and red volcanic soil were ideally suited to the cultivation of blue agave. Two of today's largest tequila brands were originally launched in the eighteenth and nineteenth centuries.

The first, Jose Cuervo, was originally produced as mezcal wine by the Cuervo family for several decades, before José María Guadalupe de Cuervo secured from the Spanish crown the first license to produce it in 1795. Then, in 1873, the Sauza family became the first distiller to call the drink made from the blue agave plant "tequila." Don Cenobio Sauza, dubbed "the father of tequila," had identified blue agave as the best variety for producing the spirit.

Agave tequilana.

AMERICA—MEET TEQUILA!

Don Cenobio Sauza was the first to export tequila to America, introducing it as *vino mescal* at the World's Columbian Exposition, aka the Chicago World's Fair of 1893. Debuting alongside Wrigley's Juicy Fruit chewing gum and Cracker Jacks, the spirit garnered a total of seven awards.

In 1916 during World War I, American troops training along the United States/Mexico border made their acquaintance with tequila in the Mexican towns of Tijuana, Juárez, Nuevo Laredo, and Matamoros. The spirit received a boost in popularity during Prohibition when *tequileros* smuggled it across the border through south Texas, and again during World War II when it was the beneficiary of decreased overseas liquor shipments.

A metal Christopher Columbus corkscrew, one of many souvenirs available at the 1893 World's Fair.

A decade later, in 1958, the spirit was cemented in the pop culture firmament with the release of "Tequila," a Latin-flavored, one-word instrumental B-side single by the Champs. It would reach number one on the *Billboard* pop chart.

Prohibition-era tequileros—tequila smugglers— could pack fifty bottles (individually wrapped in twine bags to muffle the telltale sound of clanking glass) on a single mule or donkey.

143

MEZCAL MAN

In Western literature, the greatest work of mezcal-infused fiction is Malcolm Lowry's 1947 novel *Under the Volcano*, which the author spent nearly ten years of his life writing and rewriting. *Under the Volcano* takes place on November 2, 1938, Mexico's Day of the Dead, and details the final hours of the life of Geoffrey Firmin, a British consul living in the small Mexican town of Quauhnahuac (the Nahuatl name for Cuernavaca). Firmin is a doomed alcoholic, inhabiting a mezcal-fueled dream world that plays into the myth of the spirit's psychotropic powers. For Firmin, mezcal not only numbs his pain, it serves as a conduit to moments of revelatory truth and beauty: "The drifting mists all seemed to be dancing, through the elusive subtleties of ribboned light, among the detached shreds of rainbows floating."

Written in a dense and allusive prose style, with nods to T. S. Eliot's *The Waste Land* and the daylong odyssey of Joyce's *Ulysses*, the novel sits at position 11 on the Modern Library's list of the 100 Best Novels of the twentieth century.

Malcolm Lowry's childhood hews closely to the oft-repeated story line of a young artist chafing under the restraints of a conservative, domineering father. The son of a wealthy

cotton broker, Lowry spent his formative years (1923–27) at the Leys School near Cambridge, England, the setting for James Hilton's popular novel and play *Goodbye, Mr. Chips* (1934). At school he discovered the twin passions that would govern his life—writing and booze. He is said to have begun drinking at the age of fourteen.

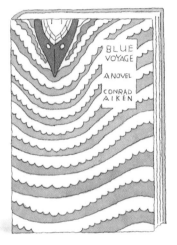

Lowry likely got his hands on this British first edition, published by Gerald Howe, London, 1927.

Later, in search of life experience, Lowry became a deckhand aboard a steamer to the Far East, before resuming his studies at St. Catherine's College in Cambridge.

The twenty-year-old Lowry sent an effusive fan letter to his idol, the American poet, novelist, and fellow tippler Conrad Aiken. This would spark a lifelong friendship between the two. The title of Lowry's first novel, *Ultramarine* (1933), was a playful reference to Aiken's 1927 novel *Blue Voyage*, a book he adored.

The Palace of Cortés in Cuernavaca, the fortified residence of conqueror Hernán Cortés, built in 1526.

On a trip to Spain with Aiken, Lowry met his first wife, an American named Jan Gabrial. They were married in France in 1934, but it was a stormy relationship, largely due to his drinking.

Two years later, following an estrangement and in a final attempt to salvage their marriage, the couple moved to the Mexican city of Cuernavaca in the state of Oaxaca.

Living in mezcal's ancestral homeland, Lowry readily availed himself of the local agave distillates. In the 1930s the spirit lacked the smoothness of modern mezcal, and in *Under the Volcano* the consul describes it as tasting "like ten yards of barbed wire fence." Unlike most drunks, Lowry was a dedicated writer when under the influence, seldom leaving a cantina without at least four pages of handwritten notes.

In another passage from *Volcano,* he describes the consul's view from his cantina barstool: "Behind the bar hung, by a clamped swivel, a beautiful Oaxaqueñan gourd of *mescal de olla,* from which his drink had been measured. Ranged on either side stood bottles of Tenampa, Berreteaga, Tequila Añejo. . . . He was safe here; this was the place he loved— sanctuary, the paradise of his despair."

His wife would walk out on him a year later. In the depths of despair, he was nonetheless writing with renewed vigor, developing what would become an early version of *Under the Volcano*. His excessive drinking eventually landed him in an Oaxacan jail, and he was subsequently deported in 1938.

Barro negro *(black clay) mezcal gourd, Oaxaca, circa 1930s.*

Margerie Bonner.

He retreated to Los Angeles, where he continued to work on drafts of *Volcano*. He hired an agent to shop the manuscript around, but it was rejected by twelve publishers. In the midst of these struggles, he met and fell in love with Margerie Bonner, an aspiring mystery writer. When Lowry's American visa expired, he crossed the border to the north, eventually settling in a squatter's cabin in Dollarton, British Colombia. Bonner soon followed, and they were married on December 2, 1940. Despite marital tensions, the nearly fifteen years the couple spent in Canada would be the happiest of Lowry's life.

J. G. Posada's Day of the Dead Calavera Oaxaqueña (Skull from Oaxaca), 1910.

Lowry devoted himself exclusively to revising his magnum opus, with considerable editorial assistance from Bonner. "We work together on it day and night," he wrote to Aiken. By the end of 1944, the final draft was complete.

Under the Volcano was finally published in 1947 to wide acclaim, and its stature would only grow with time. Lowry, hailed as a successor to Joyce, enjoyed a moment of fame but was soon lost in alcohol again. In a letter to Margerie's mother he wrote, "Success may be the worst possible thing that could happen to any serious author."

He worried that he might never write another book as good as *Volcano,* and he was right—although he continued to work on other books, he would never be published again.

The couple kicked around Europe for a year, where his drinking bouts took a darker turn—he nearly strangled Margerie in France. They returned to Dollarton in 1949, where Lowry briefly sobered up and cowrote a screenplay for F. Scott Fitzgerald's *Tender Is the Night.* MGM was interested, but the film was never produced. They left Dollarton for good in 1954, eventually settling in Sussex, England, where Lowry received treatment for his alcoholism. Margerie had to be treated for nervous exhaustion and was chronically unhappy.

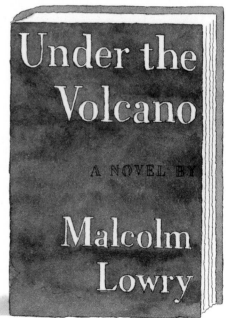

Under the Volcano

A NOVEL BY

Malcolm Lowry

First edition, Reynal & Hitchcock, New York, 1947.

Death would claim Lowry on June 26, 1957, under mysterious circumstances. His wife found his body upstairs in the cottage they were renting in the village of Ripe, and an autopsy revealed alcohol and barbiturates in his system. The coroner stated the official cause of death as "misadventure"— an accident.

The White Cottage in Ripe.

Those close to Lowry believed that suicide was out of the question. In 2004, Gordon Bowker, writing in the *Times Literary Supplement*, suggested that Margerie, after enduring years of Lowry's boorish behavior, may have played a role in his death. She had long been in the habit of plying him with vitamins to alleviate his hangovers. It would have been easy, Bowker asserted, for her to administer a fatal dose of drugs, instead of vitamins, to the unsuspecting writer.

Lowry's epitaph, which he wrote for himself, read:

> Malcolm Lowry
> Late of the Bowery
> His prose was flowery
> And often glowery
> He lived, nightly, and drank, daily,
> And died playing the ukulele.

Reflecting on his own excesses, Lowry also once wrote, "The agonies of the drunkard find their most accurate poetic analogue in the agonies of the mystic who has abused his powers."

Commemorative plaque on the White Cottage.

TEQUILA VERSUS MEZCAL

The word *mezcal* comes from the Nahuatl (the Aztec language) *mexcalli*, which means "oven-cooked agave." Mezcal is any agave-based liquor. Tequila is a type of mezcal, in the same way that scotch and bourbon are types of whiskey. Tequila must be made from blue agave, while mezcal can be made from more than thirty different varieties of agave, or maguey.

Tequila is produced in five different regions of Mexico, but primarily in a specific area surrounding the city of Tequila in the state of Jalisco. Mezcal is produced in nine areas of Mexico, with much of it being made in the state of Oaxaca. *Mescal de tequila* was the first mezcal to be codified and recognized by its geographic origin and the only one recognized internationally by its own name. Both spirits are made from the harvested core of the agave plant, or the *piña*, but they are distilled differently. Modern tequila is most often produced by slowly steaming the agave and then distilling it several times in copper pots.

A jimador harvests agave plants using his primary tool of the trade—a coa de jima (harvesting hoe). The piña, or heart of the plant, is used for production of mezcal and tequila.

Today's artisanal mezcal is made using traditional methods—the agave is wild-fermented in open vats and distilled in clay pots after being charred in underground pits. These pits are lined with lava rock and filled with wood and charcoal, imparting the distinctive smokiness for which mezcal is known.

Ron Cooper, the Southern California artist and mezcal importer credited with helping to boost mezcal's resurgence, describes the difference between steaming and charring this way: "In tequila, it's like starting with a boiled onion . . . in mezcal, it's like starting with a roasted, caramelized onion."

The esteemed Mexican writer and journalist Elena Poniatowska, when asked in a 2015 interview whether she preferred tequila or mezcal, replied, "Tequila. I'm from the old guard."

Mezcal and Tequila regions of Mexico.

CHIHUAHUA
COAHUILA
NUEVO LEÓN
DURANGO
SINALOA
ZACATECAS
TAMAULIPAS
NAYARIT
SAN LUIS POTOSÍ
Mezcal
Tequila
•Tequila
GUANA-JUATO
JALISCO
HIDALGO
MICHOACÁN
MEXICO
VERACRUZ
PUEBLA
GUERRERO
•Oaxaca
OAXACA

ON THE ROAD IN MEXICO

William "William Tell" Burroughs.

Tequila had a brief, if sordid, association with the Beat Generation. Two of the literary movement's most iconic figures, Jack Kerouac and William S. Burroughs, spent considerable

Joan Vollmer.

time south of the border. Kerouac, who once said, "Don't drink to get drunk, drink to enjoy life," enjoyed margaritas. Burroughs often drank tequila as an exotic alternate to his usual vodka and Coke.

In 1951, Burroughs and his common-law wife, poet Joan Vollmer, were living in Mexico City, where they had gotten into the habit of drinking cheap tequila throughout the day. On September 6, during a night of heavy drinking with friends, a plastered Burroughs brandished a handgun and declared to his wife, "It's time for our William Tell act." Vollmer, laughing, placed a glass of gin on top of her head. Before anyone could raise an objection, Burroughs took aim and fired, striking her in the forehead. Her death, ruled an accident, would haunt the writer for the rest of his life.

THE MARGARITA

Kerouac was likely introduced to the margarita during his 1952 bus trip from the Arizona border to Mexico City, and he would return to Mexico a half dozen times in the fifties and sixties. He told Allen Ginsberg that sitting along the coast in Mazatlán "was one of the great mystic rippling moments of my life."

Jack Kerouac.

Prior to the 1940s, few people outside of Mexico had ever heard of tequila. One of P. G. Wodehouse's characters once ordered "a shot of that Mexican drink they call—no, I've forgotten the name, but it lifts the top of your head off." The margarita would change all that.

Nobody knows for certain who invented the cocktail, but innumerable tales abound placing its origins anywhere from Acapulco, Tijuana, Ensenada, or Juárez in Mexico, to Galveston or San Diego in the United States. One popular legend maintains that it was created by Mexican restaurant owner Carlos (Danny) Herrera in 1938, for a Ziegfeld Follies showgirl named Marjorie King. She was allergic to all forms of alcohol except tequila but couldn't drink the spirit straight. To make it more palatable, Herrera added salt and lime.

Hollywood starlet Marjorie King on the cover of a vintage French tabloid magazine.

Cocktail historian David Wondrich believes the margarita evolved from a cocktail called the daisy—a popular drink in the 1930s and '40s involving gin or whiskey, citrus juice, and grenadine served over shaved ice. The original tequila daisy included orange liqueur, lime juice, and a splash of soda. The first stateside mention of a "tequila Daisy" appeared in the weekly Iowa newspaper the *Moville Mail* in 1936, by editor James Graham, who was recounting a visit to Mexico. The first appearance in print of a recipe for a drink called a "Margarita" appeared in a December 1953 issue of *Esquire*. The ever-popular frozen, or blended, margarita (anathema to purists!) owes its existence to the popular kitchen appliance used in the 1950s—the Waring blender.

The Classic (Unblended) Margarita

Ice

1 ounce Cointreau, triple sec, or other orange liqueur

2 ounces Blanco tequila

¾ ounce freshly squeezed lime juice

Kosher salt around the glass rim (optional)

Lime wedge for garnish

Add the ingredients to a shaker filled with ice and shake. Strain into a chilled cocktail glass filled with fresh ice and with salt (if using) around the rim. Garnish with a lime wedge.

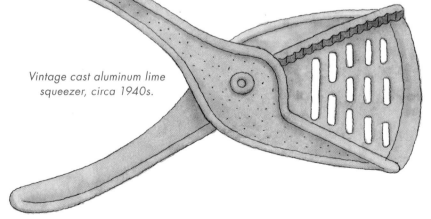

Vintage cast aluminum lime squeezer, circa 1940s.

EL BOOM

The 1960s and '70s saw an explosion of Latin American literature known as *El Boom*. One of the key figures, along with Gabriel García Márquez and Mario Vargas Llosa, was Carlos Fuentes, Mexico's grand man of letters.

In his best-known novel, *The Death of Artemio Cruz* (1964), he employs mezcal as a sort of cultural truth serum. Exposing the failed promise of the Mexican Revolution, the titular character, through a series of alcohol-induced flashbacks, remembers atrocities he committed as a young soldier in the name of the cause: "In the dark he felt for the bottle of mezcal. But it would not serve forgetfulness but to quicken memory. He would return to the beach and rocks while the white alcohol burned inside him. . . . Liquor was good for the exploding of lies, pretty lies."

Carlos Fuentes.

THE WORM

Tequila never had a worm. But certain mezcals, usually from Oaxaca, are sold *con gusano* (with worm). The worm in question is actually a moth larvae that feeds off the maguey plant, and its presence indicates an inferior product. The mezcal worm is believed to have been a marketing gimmick that began in the 1940s and 1950s to boost flagging mezcal sales in the wake of tequila's growing popularity. Spurious claims of increased virility and hallucinations after swallowing the worm only added to the mystique.

A cartoon gusano rojo ("red worm") that appears on several brands of cheap Oaxacan mezcal.

ON THE RESERVATION

Native American author Sherman Alexie, whose collection of short stories and poems *War Dances* (2009) won the 2010 PEN/Faulkner Award for Fiction, often writes of the toll alcohol has taken on the indigenous American community. Raised on the Spokane Indian Reservation in the east of Washington State in a family rife with alcoholics, he fell into the same pattern and as a college student was often drinking a fifth of tequila a day.

Sherman Alexie.

In a 2009 interview with *Big Think*, Alexie responded to a question about whether alcohol helps or hurts writers: "So there's certainly a lot to be said for my desperate years . . . my active alcoholic years as being the source of some pretty good work, for being the source of the two books that established and made my career. But the thing is, it's unsustainable. . . . If you are using substances to fuel your creativity, you're going to have a very, very short artistic life."

He stopped drinking at twenty-three.

ENTERING
Spokane Indian
Reservation

GRINGOS ON THE BORDER

Sam Shepard didn't write paeans to tequila, but he, along with his characters, was known to enjoy it. A bottle of the stuff is a constant companion for Eddie, the cowboy protagonist with a drinking problem in his 1983 play *Fool for Love*.

Cormac McCarthy drops mezcal into his punctuation-averse prose throughout his borderland novels.

Sam Shepard.

Cormac McCarthy.

In *Blood Meridian* (1985) a man's severed head is publicly displayed in a Mexican plaza floating in "a glass carboy of clear mescal." The young cowboys of *All the Pretty Horses* (1992) share many bottles of the spirit. In one scene a Mexican police captain tells a story: "I was with these boys and they have some mescal and everything—you know what is mescal?—and there was this woman and all these boys is go out to this woman and they is have this woman."

In *The Crossing* (1994), the protagonist Billy Parham refuses to drink mezcal: "You want to drink that stinkin catpiss in favor of good american whiskey . . . you be my guest."

SALT AND LIMEY

Today, agave-based liquors are riding an unprecedented wave of popularity—trendy bars and fine liquor stores offer an array of small-batch sipping tequilas and terroir-driven mezcals, aged to varying degrees of complexity and refinement. Just as sushi's growing popularity triggered the overfishing of bluefin tuna, today's mezcal boom threatens to overharvest rare, wild agave varieties.

To see how far this drink has come since its humble beginnings as a cheap corrosive for the impolite, one has only to read Kingsley Amis's notes on tequila in Every Day Drinking, *published in 1983: "Unlike other spirits, it's never advisedly drunk on its own,"* he wrote, before describing the conventional mode of consumption known to Spring-breakers everywhere: salt on the back of the left hand, lime in the right, shot glass of neat tequila at the ready.

RUM

Chapter 8

> There's nought, no doubt, so much the spirit calms, as rum and true religion.
> —Lord Byron, *Don Juan* (1819)

No spirit has seen its stock rise and fall with the frequency of rum, a drink whose reputation has alternated over the centuries and decades between cheap rotgut and elegant elixir, eventually culminating in its status as a magical mixer in the twentieth century.

American colonists couldn't get enough of it—until they decided they liked whiskey more. Rum was also all the rage at the beginning of Prohibition—until thin profit margins on the cheap spirit sent bootleggers to Canada for whiskey instead. In 1934 the resilient spirit would experience

Sacchaurum officinarum, or sugarcane.

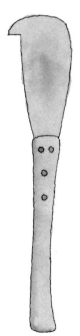

Cane knife used by plantation slaves.

another resurrection with the opening of the Hollywood restaurant Don the Beachcomber. Its Polynesian-inspired cocktail lounge, featuring rum-based tropical drinks, would introduce Tiki culture to America. The post–World War II fascination with the South Pacific helped fuel a craze that would reach its apex in the 1960s. In the intervening years Tiki's popularity has waxed and waned, with revivals in the mid-1990s and again today.

Yet despite sporadic periods of peak popularity, rum has always played second fiddle to the hard liquor triumvirate of whiskey, gin, and vodka. This is reflected in its relatively inconsequential impact on literary drinking culture.

FROM IGNOMINIOUS BEGINNINGS TO THE SEA DOG'S HAPPY DRINK

When European colonists began arriving in the Caribbean with their muskets and stills, the raw ingredients for whiskey, wine, and beer weren't readily available. It was only a matter of time before Old World distillation techniques would be pressed into service, making use of the region's plentiful local crop—sugarcane.

Plantation slave.

West Indies sugar baron.

Rum production played a central role in the Atlantic triangular slave trade from the late sixteenth to early nineteenth centuries. The drink, along with slaves, molasses, and manufactured goods, was traded between West Africa, the Caribbean, the American colonies, and Europe. This accounts for the rum's historical association with the seafaring life. Due to its wide availability, sailors and pirates operating in the Caribbean made rum their default drink of choice.

The etymology of the word *rum* is unclear, but the first distillations of fermented molasses probably took place on the sugar plantations of Barbados, a small island in the Lesser Antilles. Prior to the discovery that molasses, a byproduct of the sugar refining process, could be fermented to generate alcohol, the sticky substance was considered a waste product and a disposal headache. As rum production ramped up, molasses soon became liquid gold.

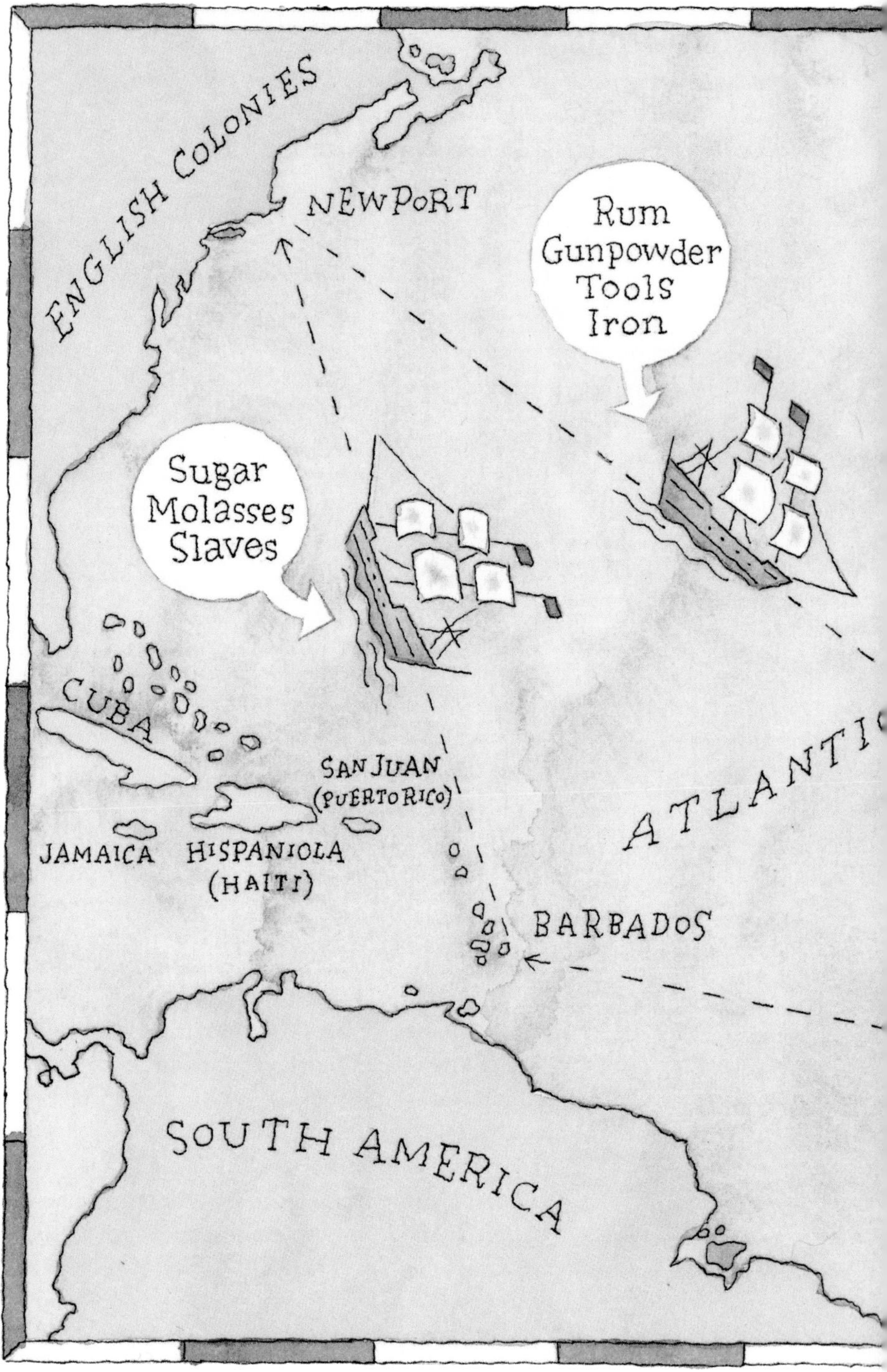
ENGLISH COLONIES
NEWPORT
Rum
Gunpowder
Tools
Iron
Sugar
Molasses
Slaves
CUBA
SAN JUAN
(PUERTO RICO)
JAMAICA
HISPANIOLA
(HAITI)
BARBADOS
ATLANTIC
SOUTH AMERICA

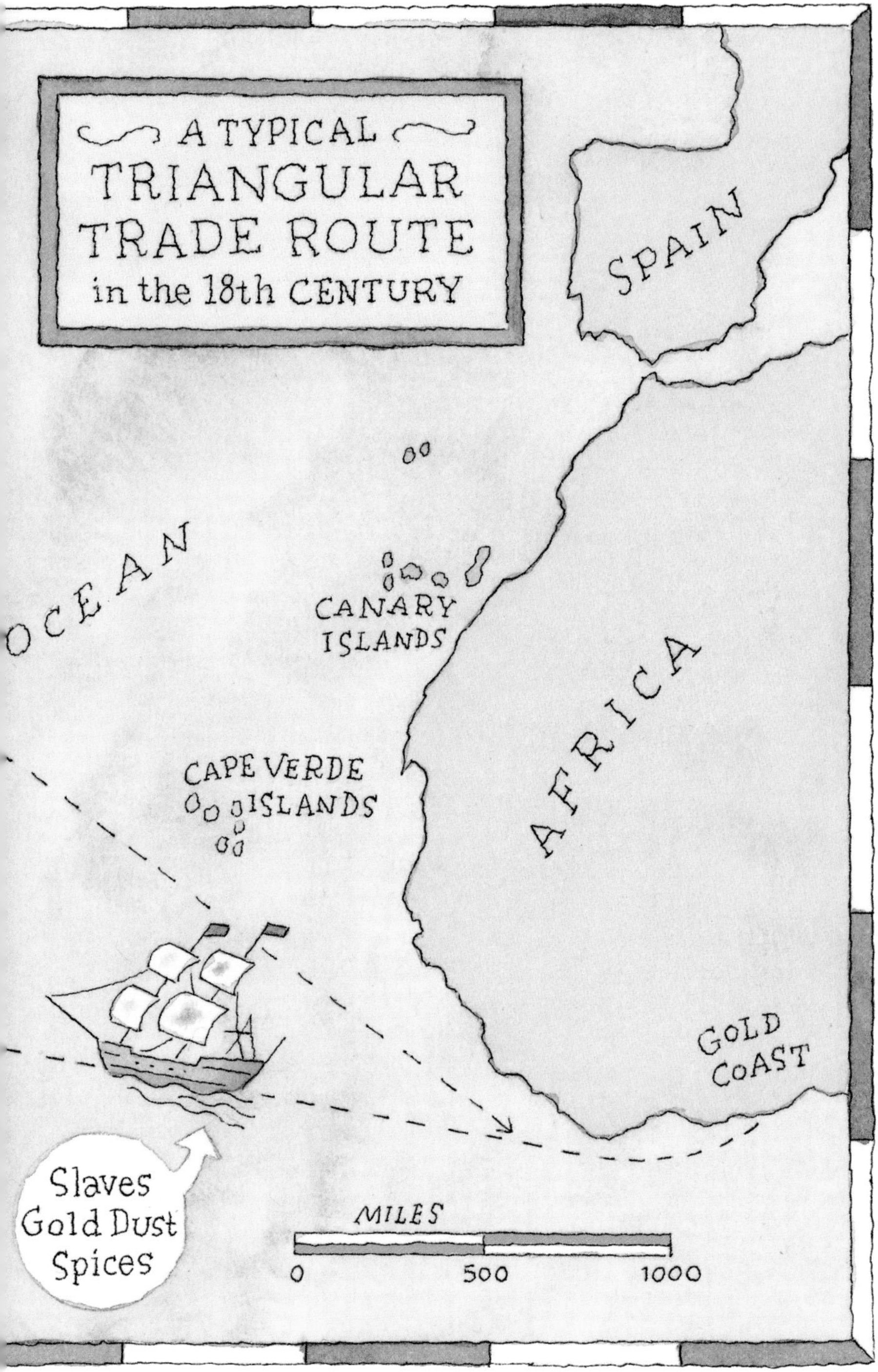
A TYPICAL
TRIANGULAR
TRADE ROUTE
in the 18th CENTURY
SPAIN
OCEAN
CANARY
ISLANDS
AFRICA
CAPE VERDE
ISLANDS
GOLD
COAST
Slaves
Gold Dust
Spices
MILES
0
500
1000

YO-HO-HO, AND A BOTTLE OF RUM!

The writer most influential in establishing the classic iconography of pirate culture, and its association with rum, was Robert Louis Stevenson.

His adventure novel *Treasure Island* (1883) had it all: treasure maps marked with an X, chests filled with loot, skull and crossbones flags, one-legged seamen with parrots perched on their shoulders, and castaways on deserted islands. And the word *rum* is mentioned more than seventy times. A 1911 edition of the novel featuring the illustrations of N. C. Wyeth further cemented Stevenson's vision in the public imagination and became the iconic *Treasure Island* read by generations of readers.

The 1911 edition with N. C. Wyeth's cover illustration, Charles Scribner's Sons, New York.

In Stevenson's time, rum was considered a crude form of alcohol (unlike the elegant wines drunk by the captain's men—and Stevenson himself). Rum is emblematic of the recklessness, self-destruction, and violence embodied by his pirates. Early on in *Treasure Island*, the ailing buccaneer Bill Bones implores the young protagonist, Jim, to fetch him "a noggin of rum" against the doctor's orders:

> "Doctors is all swabs," he said; "and that doctor there, why what do he know about seafaring men? . . . I lived on rum, I tell you. It's been meat and drink, and man and wife, to me; and if I'm not to have my rum now I'm a poor old hulk on a lee shore, my blood'll be on you, Jim, and that Doctor swab."

GROG SAVES LIVES

Eighteenth-century Royal Navy "½ gill" copper measuring cup—four cupfuls equaled a half pint, one sailor's daily rum ration.

Grog, the archetypal drink of seafarers—and a forerunner of the modern daiquiri—was the 1740 creation of Admiral Edward Vernon of the British Royal Navy. It was essentially rum drink diluted with lime juice, and served as a safeguard against scurvy, the leading cause of naval death between 1500 and 1800. Grog provided the added benefit of keeping sailors hydrated in the absence of potable water. The name came from the admiral's nickname—"Old Grog," on account of the heavy weatherproof cloak he wore made from grogram, a silk, mohair, and wool material.

RUM AND THE AMERICAN REVOLUTION

By the early eighteenth century, the New England colonies were awash in rum—the settlers were now distilling it themselves. Man, women, and children were drinking an average of three gallons of rum each year.

Unhappy with trade that was cutting into their own profits, the British enacted the so-called Sugar Act of 1764, effectively taxing any molasses imported from non-British colonies, and thereby disrupting New England's booming rum economy. This measure would only serve to inflame revolutionary passions.

TROPIC THUNDER

American writer Hart Crane was a Prohibition-era modernist poet with a taste for mai tai cocktails. He was the son of a wealthy Cleveland candy manufacturer—the inventor of Life Savers—an irony not lost on those familiar with the circumstances of the poet's death at age thirty-three.

Hart Crane.

Crane dropped out of high school at seventeen and persuaded his parents to send him to New York City, ostensibly to prepare for admission to Columbia University. Instead, he headed to Greenwich Village to make a name for himself as a poet. Ever ambitious, he proclaimed that he would "really without a doubt be one of the foremost poets in America."

Despite his overbearing father's nagging exhortations to get a real job, he managed to get published in several prestigious literary magazines, including *The Little Review* (best known for the serialization of James Joyce's *Ulysses*).

The Brooklyn Bridge inspired his collection of poetry The Bridge (1930).

Like many twentieth-century American poets, he spent a good deal of time drinking rather than writing, although he was also known to combine the two pursuits. By some accounts, he preferred to write while drunk, believing it facilitated access to the mood necessary for channeling his singular, if Delphic, vision. His inability to hold down a job for any sustained period had him shuttling back and forth between Cleveland and Manhattan for much of his late teens and early twenties.

Crane's love life was a blur of brief, often anonymous sexual encounters, mostly with men. He associated his homosexuality with his calling as a poet, using the alienation he felt, even from friends, to fuel his writing. A brief but intense relationship with a Danish sailor, Emil Opffer, inspired his poem "Voyages," written in 1924, about the redemptive power of love.

Crane was both a contributor and an ad salesman for this literary publication.

Mai tai cocktail.

The poet's love of the Caribbean—and rum—can be traced to 1926, when he relocated briefly to Cuba. His evocative poem "O Carib Isle!" invokes crabs, doubloons, terrapins, and hurricanes. In a 1927 letter to his friend Yvor Winters, American poet and literary critic, he wrote, "Rum has a strange power over me, it makes me feel quite innocent—or rather, guiltless."

His parents owned a vacation cottage on the Isle of Pines, off the Cuban coast, where he wrote most of the lyrical poems for a forthcoming volume called *The Bridge*. In a line from the book's poem "Cutty Sark," Crane invokes rum as a salve for loss:

> Murmurs of Leviathan he spoke,
> And rum was Plato in our heads . . .

In 1929 Crane left for Paris, where his emotional baggage and drunken antics followed him. He was arrested at Le Cafe Select after a physical altercation with waiters over his bar tab. He soon returned to America and completed *The Bridge*.

Publication of *The Bridge* in 1930 brought him a measure of notoriety and fame, along with some harsh critical notices. Particularly vexing for Crane were the disparaging reviews from two of his closest friends: Winters and Allen Tate (who would become the US poet laureate in 1943). This only exacerbated Crane's growing sense of himself as a failure. Along with alternating bouts of depression and elation, his drinking worsened.

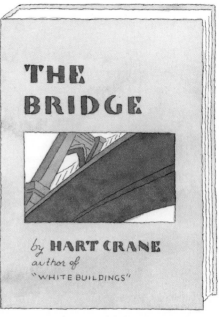

First edition, published by Horace Liveright, New York, 1930.

The Bridge would eventually be regarded by many as his crowning achievement and the greatest literary work inspired by the Brooklyn Bridge. Years later, esteemed literary critic Harold Bloom would place Crane in his pantheon of the best modernist American poets of the twentieth century. He placed *The Bridge* on equal footing with Eliot's *The Waste Land*, even regarding Crane as the superior poet.

On April 22, 1932, Crane jumped over the railing of the steamship *Orizaba*, en route from Veracruz, Mexico, to New York, in an apparent suicide. His body was never recovered.

THE DIVA OF STEEPLETOP

In 1918, Edna St. Vincent Millay was the literary "it" girl. Her celebrity transcended literary circles—she was the Madonna of her time, flouting convention and unafraid to push the boundaries of propriety. She would become the twentieth-century archetype for the artist undone by celebrity—a cautionary tale on the fleeting nature of fame and its often destructive consequences. In her day she was said to be the second-most quoted poet after William Shakespeare.

Like many writers of her day, she drank all types of liquor, but her favorite cocktail was said to be a rum-based sidecar known as between the sheets.

At age nineteen, Millay was encouraged by her mother to enter a competition sponsored by *The Lyric Year*, an annual volume of poetry. Millay's poem "Renascence," widely considered the best submission, was not awarded the top prize. The ensuing controversy made her a teenage cause célèbre.

Edna St. Vincent Millay.

While making her mark at Vassar College, Millay would sneak away from her dorm to visit Manhattan speakeasies, establishing a reputation for her drinking prowess. She was soon invited to recite her poems at literary salons around the city.

Bearing witness was Louis Untermeyer, an established American poet and critic, who remembered, "There was no other voice like hers in America. It was the sound of the ax on fresh wood." Millay graduated in 1917 with a bachelor of arts degree and moved to Greenwich Village, the center of postwar New York's burgeoning bohemian scene. That same year she published her first volume of poetry, *Renascence and Other Poems.*

A FEW FIGS
FROM THISTLES
Poems and Sonnets
By
Edna St. Vincent Millay

First edition, published by Frank Shay, New York, 1922.

A Few Figs from Thistles (1920) was her breakout success, taking her celebrity status to new heights. The book was considered controversial for its progressive feminist leanings. It contains "First Fig," one of her most famous, and prescient, poems. The short verse embodies the "live fast, die young" ethos that would epitomize the Roaring Twenties:

> *My candle burns at both ends;*
> *It will not last the night;*
> *But ah, my foes, and oh, my friends—*
> *It gives a lovely light!*

The public adored her, and her readings were cultural events. Befitting a poet-diva of the Jazz Age, she was an omnivorous drinker, a smoker, and a sexual adventurer, taking both male and female lovers. During extended reading tours across the Atlantic, she hobnobbed with Constantin Brancusi and Man Ray in Paris.

As her popularity continued to surge, she won the Pulitzer Prize in 1923 for her fourth book, *The Ballad of the Harp-Weaver.*

Among her many suitors was noted American critic, journalist, and fellow rum enthusiast Edmund Wilson, who once compiled a list of 104 terms for "drunk" in his "Lexicon of Prohibition" (1927). Wilson once proposed to her, but Millay, fearing a dreary life of domesticity with him, declined.

But Millay was, as Wilson put it, growing "tired of breaking hearts and spreading havoc." She married Eugen Boissevain, a Dutch businessman, in 1923. He was a doting husband who, in a role reversal for the period, gave up his career to help manage hers. He was unthreatened by her progressive views and apparently willing to look the other way during her numerous extramarital peccadillos.

Millay lived at 75½ Bedford Street, New York City's narrowest house, from 1923–24.

Steepletop.

Seeking refuge from the chaos of living in Manhattan, the couple bought a country home, christened "Steepletop," in upstate New York near the town of Austerlitz. There they hosted legendary parties. The grounds included an outdoor bar called "the Ruins," a spring-fed swimming pool for skinny-dipping, and a badminton court. Millay would live here for the rest of her life.

She continued to write, but by the early 1930s, the fire was starting to dim. Her work was becoming less personal and more socially conscious. Critics were growing less receptive, and her physical beauty (a key driver of her success) was on the decline. In 1936, following a car accident that left her in severe pain, she became addicted to morphine and increasingly reliant on alcohol and other drugs.

EDNA ST. VINCENT MILLAY
NOTED AMERICAN POET RESIDED
IN THIS HAMLET OF AUSTERLITZ
AT HER HOME 'STEEPLETOP'
FROM 1920 UNTIL 1950

Historical marker on Route 9 in Austerlitz, New York.

Eugen Boissevain.

Millay withdrew from friends and the public. As she became increasingly helpless in the face of her addictions, Boissevain was also her enabler, procuring drugs and alcohol upon request.

Among the artifacts in the Millay collection at the Library of Congress are itemized monthly statements from two pharmacies in Great Barrington, Massachusetts, between 1940 and 1945. These include cases of Fleischmann's gin, Taylor's vermouth, Teacher's Scotch, and Berry's rum, as well as Demerol, Nembutal, Benzedrine, and codeine. As both the quantity and quality of her writing faded, along with her fame, Millay was eventually able to ease up on the drug use but not the booze.

A commemorative stamp, issued in 1981, honoring Millay.

When her husband died suddenly of lung cancer in 1949, a grief-stricken Millay retreated from public life, seldom venturing away from Steepletop. In widowhood she became even more dependent on alcohol to get through her days.

On the morning of October 18, 1950, Millay's crumpled body, still in nightgown and slippers, was discovered at the bottom of her staircase with a broken neck after an apparent fall. She had likely been working and drinking late into the previous night. She was fifty-eight.

In her notebook, at the time of her death, she had circled in pencil the last three lines of a new poem she had just written:

I will control myself, or go inside.
I will not flaw perfection with my grief.
Handsome, this day: no matter who has died.

BETWEEN THE SHEETS

Invented during Prohibition, the between the sheets is a rum-laced variation on the classic sidecar cocktail. Its creation is usually credited to Harry MacElhone of Harry's New York Bar in Paris in the early 1930s. It's a credible assertion considering MacElhone's penchant at the time for creating provocatively named cocktails—he was also responsible for a drink called the monkey gland.

Vintage Harry's New-York Bar matchbook cover featuring Harry MacElhone's caricature.

However, cocktail mythmakers often prefer a tantalizing story to the truth: a persistent rumor was that the drink's name was coined by Edna St. Vincent Millay after some late-night drunken mischief involving Edmund Wilson and poet John Peale Bishop. True or not, many sources concur that the cocktail was among her favorites.

Between the Sheets

1 ounce light rum

1 ounce Cointreau

½ ounce lemon juice

1 ounce Cognac

Cracked ice

Lemon twist for garnish

Shake ingredients well with cracked ice, then strain into a chilled cocktail glass and garnish with the twist of lemon.

PROHIBITION RUMRUNNERS AND CUBA

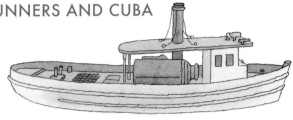

Rum smuggling has a long and colorful history dating back to the sixteenth century when pirates, evading British ships, were running the stuff from the Caribbean to the heavily taxed American colonies. The term *rumrunning* would not enter the popular lexicon until the beginning of Prohibition.

Prohibition-era rumrunner.

The risk/reward ratio was high for Prohibition smugglers. To avoid coast guard patrols, captains would run without lights at night, often through dense fog. It was not uncommon for a rumrunner to sink after hitting a sandbar or a reef, often littering a nearby shore with hundreds of rum bottles.

For Prohibition-era East Coasters, pre-Castro Cuba was a rum mecca. In 1926, to entice thirsty neighbors from the north, the Bacardi company, based in Cuba, created ad campaigns— cosponsored by Pan Am airlines—exhorting Americans to "leave the dry lands behind." Between 1916 and 1926, American travel to Cuba doubled from roughly 45,000 to 90,000 tourists a year. Havana quickly became a playground for the rich and famous, and soon a favorite destination of Ernest Hemingway.

Uncle Sam being flown from Florida to Cuba by the iconic Bacardi bat from a vintage 1920s Prohibition era ad.

175

PAPA DOBLE

A Bar La Florida 1934 cocktail menu.

Ernest Hemingway's abiding reverence for alcohol across the entire spectrum of spirits is unrivaled. But in the public imagination, the cocktail most closely identified with him is the daiquiri. After a morning workout pummeling the keys of his typewriter, Hemingway would escape the encroaching Havana heat by walking the ten minutes between his room at the Hotel Ambos Mundos to Bar La Florida (affectionately referred to by its diminutive, El Floridita), the famous Cuban watering hole.

According to the writer's niece, Hilary Hemingway, it all began in the early 1930s with a fateful call of nature. In an interview with NPR, she describes how he "went into the Floridita to use the restroom one day. People in the bar were bragging about the daiquiris that were being served there. So he ordered one and took a sip. Ernest asked for another one, this time with 'less sugar and more rum.' And that's how the *Papa Doble,* or the Hemingway daiquiri, was born." The bartender, Constantino Ribalaigua, named the modified drink in Hemingway's honor. Hemingway would become a fixture at the bar after moving to Cuba in 1932.

Constantino Ribalaigua as depicted in his 1939 cocktail menu.

In a letter to his third wife, Martha Gellhorn, in 1943, he wrote from Havana: "Everything is lovely here at the Nacional and the only thing lacking is you dear if you could only see the view from my room looking out over the beautiful gulf stream and Oh those daiquiris that nobody makes like old Constantino."

Hemingway once boasted of knocking back seventeen of Constantino's daiquiris over the course of an afternoon in 1942.

The Bacardi rum logo, circa 1900.

Papa Doble (the Hemingway Daiquiri)

Ice

2 ounces light rum (Hemingway probably drank Bacardi)

½ ounce freshly squeezed grapefruit juice

½ ounce freshly squeezed lime juice

¼ ounce maraschino liqueur

Fill a cocktail shaker halfway with ice. Add the rum, juices, and maraschino liqueur. Shake vigorously for at least 30 seconds, then strain into a chilled cocktail glass.

The daiquiri is only one of many iconic rum cocktails that enjoy popularity today, along with the mojito, the piña colada, the cuba libre, and the high-octane zombie.

The life-sized bronze statue of Hemingway installed at the end of El Floridita's bar in 2003, sculpted by Cuban artist José Villa Soberón.

YOUNG AND COMPLEX

Rum will never have the cachet, or price tag, of a fine whiskey, tequila, or red wine, because the spirit's aging process doesn't generally exceed more than a year of barrel mellowing. True to its lawless reputation, rum's provenance and production methods are largely unregulated and, as a result, quality can be all over the map.

Yet the best expressions of the sugarcane distillate can be as complex and rewarding as a fine single-malt scotch. Hemingway also enjoyed the spirit neat (as he did most of his brown liquors). In the first chapter of A Moveable Feast, *he orders himself a Saint James rum at his local café, "feeling the good Martinique rum warm me all through my body and my spirit."*

Epilogue

IT IS THE BEST OF TIMES,
IT IS THE WORST OF TIMES . . .

This present-tense modification of Charles Dickens's classic opening line from *A Tale of Two Cities* might aptly describe the state of alcohol and writing today. For the modern writer, it may seem like the worst of times. Today's authors (and publishers) must contend with the decline of print, a public that no longer reads as much as they used to, and consumers accustomed to getting their culture for free.

The intersection of the drinking life with the writing life was a product of simpler times. For writers of bygone eras who spent extended periods working in seclusion, booze was not only a muse but also an antidote to loneliness, depression, anxiety, and stress. The fraught process of creating a book with a large publisher was not for the faint of heart, with its share of setbacks and detours that had authors reaching for the bottle on more than a few occasions.

Drink was also an excuse to get away from the typewriter and commune at the local watering hole with kindred spirits. Today, in the age of social media, decentralized cultural centers, and pharmaceutical abundance, the typical modern writer (with certain exceptions) no longer hangs out in bars and has likely supplanted alcohol with the chemical support of Adderall, Zoloft, or medicinal marijuana.

For the modern drinker, however, it is the best of times. The sheer number of quality offerings available today in every spirit category is unparalleled in history. And to help navigate the sea of booze, the savvy dipsomaniac with a smartphone can pull up spirit reviews and buying advice on the fly, while browsing the aisles of the local liquor emporium. The "ombibulous" H. L. Mencken, a man who enjoyed all manner of drink, wouldn't have known where to start.

We hope you've enjoyed the spirituous and literary abundance in these pages. As always, please drink—and read—responsibly.

—*Greg Clarke* and *Monte Beauchamp*

ACKNOWLEDGMENTS

I owe the existence of this book to Monte Beauchamp, who approached me with the idea of collaborating on an illustrated history involving booze, writers, artists, and musicians (Dey St. wisely suggested we narrow the scope!).

I'm exceedingly grateful to my wife, Jenifer Leonard; my daughter Greta; and my son Julian for putting up with the twelve months where I was effectively an absentee husband and father.

And a special thanks to our agent, Gillian McKenzie; our editors Jessica Sindler and Sean Newcott; our legal counsel Victor Hendrickson; Alivia Lopez; Suet Yee Chong; and the entire team at Dey St.

—*Greg Clarke*

A deep-hearted thanks to my collaborator and friend Greg Clarke, and to Gillian, Jessica, Victor, Sean, Alivia, Suet and the remainder of the team at HarperCollins / Dey Street for helping shepherd this book through to fruition. A very special thanks to the remarkable Rebecca Hall for her unconditional support throughout the two-year journey.

—*Monte Beauchamp*

From left: Monte Beauchamp, the Boozehound, and Greg Clarke.